AMERICAN PHILOSOPHICAL QUARTERLY
MONOGRAPH SERIES

AMERICAN PHILOSOPHICAL
QUARTERLY
MONOGRAPH SERIES

BF 311
.S735

Edited by NICHOLAS RESCHER

STUDIES IN THE
PHILOSOPHY OF MIND

Essays by:

Harold Brown
Haskell Fain and
  A. Phillips Griffiths

O. H. Green
Donald F. Henze
Moreland Perkins

Alan R. White

Monograph No. 6   Oxford, 1972

PUBLISHED BY BASIL BLACKWELL

© *American Philosophical Quarterly 1971*
ISBN 0 631 11500 5

Library of Congress Catalog
Card No.: 79–190091

PRINTED IN ENGLAND
by C. Tinling & Co. Ltd., London and Prescot

CONTENTS

EDITOR'S PREFACE

The present volume extends the series of monographs published under the auspices of the *American Philosophical Quarterly* to its sixth number. It is fitting that its theme should be the philosophy of mind, this being among the most active branches of the discipline in the English-language orbit. The *American Philosophical Quarterly* is grateful to the authors for committing their contributions to this volume.

The editor wishes to thank his wife for assistance in seeing the book through the press.

Nicholas Rescher
Pittsburgh
September, 1971

Perception and Meaning
HAROLD BROWN

I

ONE of the central concerns of philosophical discussions of perception is the attempt to clarify the nature of the perceptual object, i.e., the attempt to characterize the sort of object that we literally see, hear, touch, taste, or smell. Theories of the sense-datum variety, for example, maintain that the proper objects of perception are pure sensory atoms of color and shape, sound, etc., which are private to the individual percipient and totally indubitable. But the sense-datum theorist, like any other theorist, does not develop his theory of perception as a result of an examination of perception carried out from the standpoint of wide-eyed innocence. Rather, before he begins any examination of cases of perception he already has a general view as to what role perception plays in human knowledge and experience, some fairly specific questions about the nature of perception that he is attempting to answer within this framework, and a more or less explicit set of criteria for what constitutes an acceptable answer to these questions. This is not a criticism of the sense-datum theorist, of course, but rather a fundamental, and I hope familiar, point about the structure of inquiry: if we have no beliefs at all about the subject matter at hand we have no reason to ask any questions about it and no grounds for evaluating any claims. In the case of the sense-datum theorist the starting point of the inquiry into perception can be stated as follows: (1) He is attempting to carry out the empiricist program of founding all knowledge on perception, and (2) he believes that if there is any genuine knowledge at all its foundations must be indubitable.

Alternative characterizations of the perceptual object emerge when one begins from a different starting point. One might, for example, have reasons for rejecting the empiricist program and replacing it with the thesis that all knowing involves conceptual processes and that perception is a form of knowing. Clearly, working from this starting point, the proper objects of perception will not turn out to be pure sensory atoms. And one can also develop an alternative to a theory by another route that does not involve the

1

explicit, initial denial of its starting point. Rather, we can follow out the consequences of a theory until we reach an aspect of our subject matter that the theory in question cannot adequately deal with and then take that aspect as the new starting point. The sense-datum theorist, for example, has considerable difficulty in accounting for the apparently public nature of so many of the objects that we perceive and we can thus take the thesis that the objects of perception are public as a new starting point for the development of an alternative characterization of the percept. This is, in effect, what has been done by those contemporary writers on perception who maintain that the proper objects of perception are material objects, i.e., entities which are not private to any conscious being, but which exist in their own right independently of any mind and which can be perceived by any being who is equipped with the proper sense organs.

In this paper I will reconsider the nature of the perceptual object from a different starting point than any of those mentioned above and will thus develop yet another characterization of the perceptual object. Our starting point will be the thesis that the primary function of perception is to provide us with information about the things and events in the world around us and we will begin by considering some instances in which perception does supply such information. I am not, however, merely attempting to add one more description of the percept to the philosophical catalogue, for I will, in the course of the paper, try to show why neither the sense-datum nor the material object of characterization of the percept can account adequately for cases of significant perception. It must also be emphasized that our concern in this paper is limited to a consideration of the perceptual object in so far as it is a source of information, i.e., we will limit ourselves to an epistemic characterization of the perceptual object. But although nothing will be said here about the ontological status of percepts, it should be clear that if our analysis is adequate any future attempt to consider the ontological status of the percept will have to be consistent with our results.

II

The central characteristic of those cases in which perception serves as a source of information is that they involve the identification of the objects or events that are being perceived. To see a table or the letter F or the path of an electron in a cloud chamber, to hear a horse or a typewriter, to smell sulphur dioxide, etc., are all cases in which perception supplies me with information about the world around me.

But it is a source of information exactly because I succeed in identifying these objects. Seeing an unrecognizable streak in an unfamiliar gadget will not help the physicist to confirm or reject any physical hypothesis nor will hearing assorted clicks tell me anything about what is happening in the next room nor will smelling an odor which I cannot place tell me anything about what is happening to my environment. But a given object can be subject to a variety of different identifications and thus supply different sorts, and perhaps even different degrees, of information. Thus the person who, in the presence of sulphur dioxide, recognizes only the smell of rotten eggs does not obtain the same information as one who recognizes the smell of sulphur dioxide and understands the chemistry of this gas and its significance as a pollutant. Similarly, to recognize the sound of a typewriter gives me some information about what is happening in the next room, but suppose that I also happen to know that the occupant of the next room is an aspiring novelist who had been having difficulties with his writing and who had, only yesterday, sworn that he would never write again. In the latter case hearing the sound of the typewriter would give me a great deal more information than in the former case.

As the above examples illustrate, different individuals can obtain different information in a given perceptual situation and the sort of information that an individual obtains depends on the nature of the knowledge that he brings with him into that perceptual situation. Now it would certainly not be an uncommon use of language to describe these differences by saying that a given perceptual situation can have a different meaning to different individuals. But the information that an individual gleans from a given case of perception is identical with the meaning that that situation has for him and, in so far as perception functions as a source of information, the object of perception is this meaning.

Undoubtedly, many philosophers will find the suggestion that we perceive meanings odd. Thus I will attempt, in what follows, to alleviate this feeling of oddity. Since it is a relatively non-controversial thesis that we do find meaning in language, it will be helpful to consider what is involved in grasping the meaning of written or spoken language.

III

The first point that must be made about the communication of meaning through language is that it is always based on perception.

In order to grasp the meaning of a written text I must see it (or, in the case of braille, feel it) and in order to grasp the meaning of a speech I must hear it. But this is not to be taken as suggesting that we are dealing with two temporally distinct steps—I do not first hear a sound or see a mark from which I then extract a meaning. Rather, to read a text or to hear a speech in a language which I understand is to be conscious of a meaning throughout. Let us consider these cases somewhat more closely.

From one point of view, a printed text is nothing but a series of marks on paper, but it is never this from the point of view of an individual who is reading the text in question. For such an individual each sign-design has a meaning and it is this meaning that he is concerned with. But "having meaning" is not a monadic property of the printed mark itself, it is a relative property. A sign-design only has meaning when it is seen by an individual who has the knowledge that is necessary to grasp a meaning. To be clear on this point it is sufficient to note that a series of marks such as "man" will have no meaning for an illiterate or for a person who only reads Hebrew, but it will have a meaning for someone who reads English and a different meaning for someone who reads German. And it will convey yet another, and perhaps a much richer meaning, to someone for whom this word is a coded message.

The parallels between this case and the examples of perception that were mentioned earlier should be clear. A given page or a given object has a meaning for me if I approach it with the necessary information and it can have different meanings for different people. And, just as I must learn to read, so I must learn to grasp the meaning of the objects that I perceive. We do not appear in the world any more capable of recognizing the odor of rotten eggs than the odor of a highly corrosive, poisonous gas. Even to recognize as simple an object as a table requires that we have learned to perceive in a particular way, in a particular culture. An individual who came from a culture in which there were no tables and who had never before encountered anything like our tables would not see a table when he looked at this object. (Although this does not prevent those of us who are from our culture from describing him, to each other, as looking at and seeing the table.) Similarly, an individual who came from a culture that did not use tables as we use them but which did use objects that look just like our tables for, say, certain ritual purposes only, would see something different from what I see when he looked at my table, just as one who reads only German sees a different word than I do when he looks at "man." The ways in which a printed page and a perceived object have meaning for a person are, then, sufficiently similar to allow us to conclude that if it is correct to say that the objects that we read are meanings, then it is equally correct to say that we perceive meaning.

Undoubtedly, an objection will be raised at this point, i.e., that although it may be correct to say that we read meanings, it is not correct to say that we see meanings when we read. Rather, it will be maintained, the process of reading needs a different sort of analysis, one which recognizes that we see some object (not a meaning) printed on the page and that it is as a result of seeing this object that we grasp a meaning. (The objection need not be taken as proposing that there are two temporally distinct processes involved here, but rather two logically distinct processes.) But this only returns us to a new version of our original problem, i.e., the objector must now offer a characterization of this object that the reader sees. If I do not see meanings when I read, then what is it that I do see? We cannot say that I see a word and then grasp its meaning, for to recognize a perceived object as a word is to view this object in terms of a language system. If I have no familiarity with language at all, I will not see a word in any circumstances; and if I read English but do not even know of the existence of languages which use other alphabets, I will not see any words when I look at a Greek text. Thus the suggestion that I see words and grasp meanings will not work because to see a word is to recognize an object and thus to grasp a meaning and this first attempt to distinguish between seeing a word and grasping a meaning fails.

The obvious next step in the regress towards a pure object of seeing would be to suggest that what we see is a collection of letters, but this attempt fails for the same reason that the previous attempt failed. Even if I do not recognize what letters I am dealing with, I still grasp a meaning when I recognize that these objects are letters, since I am still perceiving in the context of a language. If I were totally unfamiliar with written language, I would not see letters.

The next step, perhaps, will be to say that we see marks printed on a page or perhaps sign-designs, but even here we must be able to recognize these marks as a special sort of mark or sign-design if they are to serve as the perceptual basis for reading a text. Thus we are still dealing with recognized objects and, as we have seen, whenever we recognize an object we are grasping a meaning. The objector's task, it will be recalled, is to attempt to locate some perceptual object which is not itself meaningful but which serves as a foundation from which I grasp meanings. Clearly, any example which is itself the grasping of a meaning will not serve this purpose and in order to completely eliminate the presence of meaning from our examples we must move down to a point at which we are no longer dealing with a recognizable object, but at this point we no longer have an object which can serve as a basis for grasping a meaning, for how can we grasp the meaning of totally unrecognized object? In the case of reading, then, the attempt to make a distinction between the meaning of what we read and the object that we actually see has failed and we can conclude that when we read we see meanings.

Returning, now, to the case of perception, essentially the same argument holds. To recognize an object is to be aware of a meaning and we cannot divide any cases of perception into a pure perceptual substratum and a meaning which is grasped as a result of our perception of this substratum. Either the substratum is a recognizable object in which case we are still grasping a meaning and the division in question remains to be made, or it is not a recognizable object in which case it cannot serve as a foundation for the grasping of a meaning.

Since the above argument gives, in effect, a reason why sense-datum type descriptions of the percept are not adequate to account for the role that perception plays as a source of information, it will be helpful to consider, at this point, the other description of the percept that was mentioned at the beginning of the paper, i.e., the thesis that we do not perceive anything nearly so unsubstantial as meanings, but rather that we perceive material objects.

In response to this claim let us first note that we do not perceive only material objects. When, for example, I see a rainbow or a mirror image or hear a clap of thunder or a speech I am not perceiving a material object. Let us consider, then, some of the characteristics of those cases in which we do perceive material objects.

To perceive a material object is not merely to be aware of an object having a certain size, shape, color, etc., but it is also to have a particular body of expectations about this perceived object. This body of expectations includes such things as the expectation that if I close my eyes and open them again I will see the same object that I saw before, that if I am close enough to it I will be able to touch it, that if I were to walk around behind it it would not vanish but would have another side, and the like. These are expectations which, as a result of prior learning, I have in certain perceptual situations and do not have in others. I do not expect to feel flesh when I reach out and touch the person in the mirror nor do I expect to find someone behind the mirror. For an adult who has been brought up in a culture in which mirrors are common, the knowledge that there is no one behind the mirror is part of the information that he obtains when he recognizes that he is looking in a mirror and the knowledge that the table has a back is also included in my recognition of it. These are all things that I have learned to recognize just as I have learned to recognize a typewriter or sulphur dioxide. Thus the fact that I am confronted with a material object is part of the information about my environment that I can derive from perception if I bring a certain body of relevant information into the perceptual situation with me. If I do not have this prior information I will not recognize a material object and, from the point of view that concerns us, I will not perceive a material object. Thus the fact that we do perceive and recognize material objects does not stand as a counter-instance to the thesis that we perceive meanings, but rather as one more example of thrust of this thesis.

Spoken language differs from written language in that, by means of inflection, tone of voice, or the like, it has additional means of conveying meaning that written language does not possess. But even including these additional means of expression, the same points hold that were made in the case of written language. Spoken language can only function as a source of information if I know the relevant language and can thus grasp the meaning of what is being said and a tone of voice can only convey information if I recognize that tone. A given sound or tone can have different meanings for different people and thus convey different bodies of information to different people and no information at all to some, depending on the sort of information that they already have available before they hear the sound. And a bare, unidentified sound can convey no information at all. It is this last point, once again, that is the main point of our discussion, for it holds equally of all sounds, not only of those sounds that have been selected out for use in a particular language. On this score there is no difference between the utterances of a university lecturer and the roar of a jet plane. If hearing the sounds is a source of information to the hearer, then it is because these sounds are meaningful to him and the object of his perception is the meaning of these sounds.

In order to emphasize further the point that there is no significant difference between the role that meaning plays in cases of reading or listening to language on the one hand and all other forms of perceiving on the other, let us consider two series of perceptual situations, one auditory, and one visual. In each case I am about to cross a set of railroad tracks when I perceive the object in question. First, the auditory series: (1) the shouted statement, "Do not cross now, a train is coming!" (2) A ringing bell; (3) The sound of a train whistle;

(4) The sounds of the wheels of a train on the tracks. Secondly, the visual series: (1) A sign that lights up and says, "Do not cross now, a train is coming!" (2) A flashing red light; (3) Black smoke from around a curve; (4) The sight of a train. Both of these sets begin with linguistic objects followed by examples of more or less conventional warning signs, and end with what we would normally describe as hearing or seeing a train. In all of these cases I must recognize the object before me in order to glean any information on the basis of which to act and if I do not already have the necessary body of information, whether it be a knowledge of the language, of the relevant conventions, or of what a train is, I might act in a rather unfortunate manner—as might a person from an alien culture or a child from our own culture. And there are no grounds for dividing either of these series into two classes, one which includes all cases in which the percipient grasps a meaning and one which includes those cases in which he simply sees or hears an object. In each case the percipient gains information if he recognizes the objects before him, i.e., if he grasps their meaning, and whether he grasps their meaning or not depends on what he already knows.

IV

There is yet one more question that I want to examine in closing. Suppose that it is granted that the objects of significant perception are meanings, what conclusions follow about the ways in which perception functions as a source of knowledge? One conclusion is clear. We have seen that a given perceptual situation can convey more meaning to one individual than to another and that how much information is conveyed depends on how much the percipient already knows. From this it follows that the more we know, the more we can learn from perception and that the more naive the percipient is, the less he can learn from any given case of perception. This is clear from our examples: the individual who reads a book or listens to a lecture will find more meaning in it the more he knows about the subject just as the chemist who recognizes sulphur dioxide learns a lot more about his environment than the person who only knows about rotten eggs. The point is most clearly illustrated in the case of the sciences, for a person who knows nothing about the discipline in question can learn nothing at all by observing an experiment—indeed, he might not even know that an experiment was going on. And the scientist himself can learn more from his experiment the more fully familiar he is with the details and implications of his theories. A scientist who has not carried the deductive elaboration of his theories far enough might be totally unable to grasp the meaning of an event which, for another scientist, would serve to confirm or disconfirm a theory.

Finally, it should be noted that this conclusion is directly contrary to the tradition in epistemology which wishes to construct knowledge out of indubitable bits of hard data—colored patches, pointer readings, etc. It is not by making minimal observations and taking minimal conceptual risks in describing them that we increase our knowledge, but rather by bringing to bear the full force of everything that we already know or believe about the situation at hand. In this way the meaning of each perceptual situation is enriched and the possibility of perception acting as a check on our existing beliefs or as a source of new information is increased.

Northern Illinois University

On Falsely Believing That One Doesn't Know

HASKELL FAIN AND
A. PHILLIPS GRIFFITHS

THERE is no proposition so transparent in its falsehood that all of mankind could see through it. There is no proposition so compactly true that no one could miss it. The most trivial of tautologies can be believed false; the most blatant of contradictions can be believed true. Even that most venerable proposition "I exist"—which, Descartes claimed, is "necessarily true each time that I pronounce it, or that I mentally conceive it"—can be falsely believed to be false. For what is to prevent some lunatic from believing that he does not exist? The principle of unlimited gullibility, as we shall call it, seems everywhere applicable: any false proposition can be falsely believed by someone to be true; any true proposition can be falsely believed by someone to be false. What does it mean, in particular, to believe falsely that one does not know that p? Simply this. One believes one does not know that p when it is true one does know that p all along.

It should come as no surprise that the principle of unlimited gullibility is itself quite capable of being believed—falsely, we believe—to be false. For one thing, under ordinary circumstances, it conflicts with the conjunction of two principles commonly found in epistemological theory, namely: If one knows that p, then one knows that one knows that p; if one knows that p, then one believes that p. No one who accepted both these principles could accept the principle of unlimited gullibility as it applies to true propositions of the form: I know that p. For suppose it were possible for Smith to believe, falsely, that he did not know some proposition p. Then Smith would be in the position of believing that he did not know that p, though *he did know that p* all the while. If Smith believes that he does not know that p, then, if rational, he certainly will not believe that he knows that p. If knowing implies believing, then if Smith does not believe that he knows that p, he does not know that he knows that p. And if knowing implies knowing that you know, then if Smith does not know that he knows that p, then he does not know that p either.

10

But if Smith can *falsely* believe that he does not know that p, then he must know that p after all. Some principle or other has to give way.

Our aim here is not to pick a dry bone with these oft-mentioned though by no means universally accepted epistemological principles. The main target is philosophical skepticism which we shall take to be the position that no one knows anything at all. The main varieties of philosophical skepticism all seem to be based, in one way or another, upon the claim that man is fallible without limit. From this claim, the skeptic proceeds, via the apparently plausible principle that knowing that p implies knowing that one is not mistaken about the truth-value of p, to the conclusion that one does not know any p at all. For, if man is fallible, who knows that he is not mistaken on any particular occasion about the truth-value of some particular p? We shall contend presently that this latter thesis is completely mistaken—that having knowledge is not only compatible with the abstract possibility of being mistaken, but with the concrete knowledge that one may be mistaken and is even compatible with the conviction that one *is* mistaken in supposing that p. Before getting down to cases, however, it is interesting to compare the principle of unlimited fallibility, upon which the skeptic relies, with what we termed "the principle of unlimited gullibility." The principle of unlimited fallibility maintains that for all propositions p, and all persons x, x could be mistaken about the truth-value of p. The principle of unlimited gullibility can be recast as saying that for every proposition p, there exists at least one person x, who could be (gulled into being) mistaken about the truth-value of p. It will be seen that the principle of unlimited fallibility implies the principle of unlimited gullibility, but not vice versa.

Philosophers, following Descartes, usually attempt to refute philosophical skepticism by attacking the principle of unlimited fallibility. They maintain that there exists at least one proposition (e.g., "I exist," "It seems to me that I see light") and at least one person—namely, themselves—such that it is absurd to suppose that that person could be mistaken about the truth-value of that particular proposition. Some philosophers, following G. E. Moore, attempt to answer the skeptic by vigorously denying that they ever *are* mistaken with regard to many of the propositions about which the skeptic claims they can be mistaken. Both these kinds of strategies are aimed directly at defeating the principle of fallibility and, to the extent they are successful, block the most important route, historically speaking, followed by philosophical skepticism. However, neither strategy tells against the principle of gullibility; though Descartes may have shown that he could not have been mistaken *in his own case* about the truth-value of "I exist", he certainly did not show that no one could be mistaken about the truth-value of "I exist" as it applied in *his* own case.

Our arguments will show that the principle of gullibility is true, at least as it applies to propositions of the form "*S* knows that *p*." The skeptic, believing that the principle of fallibility is true is committed, willy-nilly, to the principle of gullibility as well. Since we are in agreement with the skeptic concerning the truth of the principle of gullibility, it might appear that we are giving aid and comfort to the enemy denied him by those who claim that it is logically impossible to believe falsely that one does not know. It is easy to show, however, that the skeptic is afforded quite a surprising advantage if one concedes that impossibility. For suppose that it were logically impossible to believe falsely that one did not know. Now the philosophical skeptic believes that no one, including himself, knows anything at all. Accordingly, it must be true that he knows nothing. So much the worse for him, you might say. Ah, but skeptics are indefatigable proselytizers. Suppose, then, that by outrageously bad arguments, the skeptic persuades Smith that Smith knows nothing. If Smith cannot falsely believe he knows nothing, then directly that he believes he knows nothing, he ceases to know anything at all. And so on, for all the Smiths of mankind, until no one indeed knows anything and philosophical skepticism is vindicated. Still, the truth of the proposition that no one knows anything ought to be quite independent of whether the skeptic manages to convince mankind of its truth. It ought to be *possible* to believe falsely that one does not know anything even when one really does know a thing or two. Otherwise, what would be the point of arguing with a skeptic, convinced as he is that no one knows anything? In short, it is necessary to show that the skeptic *can* be wrong, even about his own case, before setting about to show that he is in fact wrong in thinking that no one knows anything. To do this, one must argue that anyone, including the skeptic, can falsely believe that he does not know. Let us, accordingly, proceed to the argument.

Imagine an ordinary man set the ordinary task of doing ten simple arithmetic sums. Each problem is not much more complicated than, say, adding 35 to 87. The man, Smith, is asked to take his time, to check as often as he likes until he knows the answer to each problem. We may pedantically recast the situation as one in which Smith is asked to make ten assertions, each one having the form "I know that P_1," "I know that P_2" . . ., "I know that P_{10}" where each of the P's, corresponding to each of ten addition problems is a sentence such as "$35+47=82$." If the word "know" has any application at all, it ought to have application here. True, most people do not usually discriminate between being simply asked what the answer to each problem is, and being asked if they *know* what that answer is. Few will see much difference between asserting "35+47=82" and asserting "I know that 35+47=82" in situations such as those we are considering. Indeed, one may think this fact provides support for contending that the word "know" in such situations has no real application, since it is readily eliminated without any apparent loss of content in what is being communicated by the person who says "35+47=82" rather than "I *know* that 35+47=82." And if the word "know" does not appear are knowledge claims nonetheless, inasmuch logical bearing. This argument, however, can be turned inside out. One can just as well maintain that many assertions in which the word "know" does not appear are knowledge claims nonetheless, inasmuch as speakers see little to choose between asserting "I know that *p*" and asserting '*p*.'

The moral, of course, is that the occurrence or lack of the word "know" in statements drawn from everyday discourse is not of itself sufficient to establish or deny epistemological relevancy. One must take into careful account the context and situation of the speaker. Suppose, for example, one is set the task of calculating, mentally, the sum of three five-digit numbers. Few people would choose to say that they *knew* the answer, though a good number might get it right. The point is that the addition of simple sums, with pencil and paper, are just the sorts of cases in which the word "know" is directly applicable; so much so that few speakers will understand what more is being asked of them when they are required to make knowledge claims in place of simply stating the answers. Are we requesting that they do their sums more than once or twice? We are not requiring that they be sure so much as sure-footed in matters arithmetical, and most people check their sums once or twice as a matter of course.

Our man Smith soon performs his simple calculations and is prepared to humor us by making ten knowledge claims. Smith knows that P_1, Smith knows that P_2, and so on. And why shouldn't he? Except that poor Smith, we discover, has made a mistake with respect to P_7. He thinks that 75 added to 57 makes 133. Ever since reading Kant, Smith has had a hang-up about sevens and fives although, let us suppose, he is unaware that he is arithmetically kinky in this way. Suppose, upon our informing him that 75+57=132, he rechecks his addition and, thoroughly embarrassed, agrees with us. The situation is a perfectly normal one. Since P_7, "75+57=133," is false, Smith cannot know that P_7, though he *thought* he did before we pointed our his error. Would anyone suppose that because Smith made one mistake with regard to P_7, he does not really know the rest of his P's? (What would you say if a teacher claimed your child did not know any of the answers on an arithmetic test because he made a mistake on one of them?)

Let us now change the situation a little. Suppose we inform Smith that he has made one mistake. This time, however, we do not show him his mistake but simply tell him that he has made one. Smith, remember, is peculiar where sevens and fives are concerned and so it is not difficult to conjecture that no matter how many times he checks his calculations, he never discovers his mistake in P_7. We expect Smith to check his calculations upon being apprised of an error. So should any rational man. But what ought to be Smith's attitude when he is not only aware of the possibility of error, but is informed by an authority that he has made one, an error he himself is unable to discover?

Personality differences can come into play at this point. The situation we have conjured up is not unlike the conditions introduced during certain socio-physical and psycho-physical perception experimentation. The victim is typically subjected to a barrage of misinformation, group displeasure and the like, all of which is designed to get him to change his mind about matters which are initially as plain to him as the nose on his face. For the unsuspecting, in fact, experiments of these kinds are extremely harrowing. Those victims who manage to avoid looking like utter idiots are usually bull-headed types who shout down their tormenters. They know, damn it, and the rest of the world can go to blazes. Though stubbornness of this kind can, on certain occasions, earn our applause, should it serve as the very model of what it means to know that something is the case?

Suppose that our man Smith, goaded by his inability to discover his error, turns around and attempts to bully us into thinking that it is we who are wrong. By standing firm, he gives us no ground for saying that he does not know the other nine propositions. And yet, we are not attempting, as with the victim of a psycho-physical perception experiment, to deceive Smith; though we may drive him mad. Suppose, on the other hand, that Smith were the kind of victim who goes to pieces when subjected to group pressure. It is quite possible that, under severe conditions, one can literally forget how to add. But should it always be so shocking to suppose that one was wrong in thinking that one knew; so shocking that all one's knowledge flew out of the window? True, for some kinds of people, the mere belief that they do not know provides sufficient ground for saying

that they do not know. Yet is this the case for all of us, as the ortho-
dox epistemologist will want to claim it *must* be? Is there no middle
course between the gnostic bully and the agnostic milksop?

Let us begin by inquiring whether Smith ought to claim that he
knows that P_1, that he knows that P_2, and so on while in the position
of publicly accepting as fact that he has made one mistake. Is it
still a principle of rational discourse that one ought not to advance
inconsistent claims? If so, then Smith ought not to claim that he
knows that P_1, that he knows that P_2, etc., the while maintaining that
one of the P's is false. Even so, the fact that one ought not *to claim*
knowledge on certain occasions is not a sufficient condition for
denying its existence. There are all sorts of reasons for holding one's
tongue, for refusing to hunt wild ducks. And yet, surely, there has
to be some mode of describing Smith's epistemic predicament in a
consistent manner.

Suppose that instead of claiming that he knew each of the P's,
Smith made a disjunctive knowledge claim: I know that P_1, or I
know that P_2, or . . ., or I know that P_{10}. Smith could then claim,
consistently, that one and only one of the P's was false. The two
claims, together, can give a fair representation of Smith's epistemic
situation. The disjunctive knowledge claim is true even if one of the
disjuncts is false.

Which disjunct? Smith may never discover that P_7 is false—he
may never find out that he did not know that P_7. That, in itself, is
no cause for alarm. What is a little curious—curious until one gets
used to the idea—is that we know that Smith knows that the other
P's are true, though Smith himself is not privy to that second-order
knowledge. And yet, should that point really be so hard to ac-
knowledge? Don't successive generations vet the knowledge claims
of predecessors from new vantage points? The growth of knowledge
is not a simple additive process taking place on the same level.

We claim, then, that the case of Smith provides a hypothetical but
genuine example of knowing that a certain proposition is true without knowing that one knows it. Smith may, in fact, believe—falsely—
that he does not know that P_1. Perhaps the problem corresponding
to P_1 is different from the others in that it involves three-column
instead of two-column addition. Smith may suppose, quite reason-
ably, the greater the number of columns and rows, the more the
likelihood of going astray in adding them, and thereby conclude that
he does not know that P_1 simply on the basis of probabilities.

Suppose, then, this conjecture leads Smith to deny vigorously that
the answer to the first problem is stated by P_1, and that it is in fact

anything but P_1. Though we are not committed to the familar epistemological view that knowing implies believing, it may well be that in *this* case Smith's total abandonment of his original answer would require us to say that he no longer knows that P_1. But is this analysis of Smith's state of affairs the only one possible? Smith's belief that P_1 is false is emotionally compatible with a considerable attachment to it. Though Smith's two convictions are inimical, there is nothing logically self-contradictory about describing him as possessing both of them at the same time. Surely, then, a fair way of describing Smith's position, under the circumstances, is that he falsely believes that he does not know that P_1. Have we taken advantage of an odd and extraordinary situation to press an odd and extraordinary description of it? No. As long as Smith does not abandon the principles of arithmetic, we need not be overly disturbed if his case appears to impugn the principles of an overly-rationalistic psychology. He is, after all, quite a reasonable creature, having found the middle course between gnostic bullishness and agnostic milksoppery. Indeed, Smith's state of mind is not unfamiliar to anyone who has ever encountered counter-intuitive results in mathematics. Smith's knowledge, then, of having made one mistake does not rob him of his first order knowledge. And if the virtual existence of error is compatible with first order knowledge, so is it the case with the abstract possibility of error. The skeptic needs more than the truth of the principle of unlimited fallibility to prove his thesis.

It is, then, possible falsely to believe that one does not know, and hence to know may not be to know that one knows. But now, what possible use is such knowledge to anybody? Can we congratulate ourselves on possessing the elixir, when its phial is indistinguishable from those containing poisons?

Certainly, our imaginary calculator's knowledge is of no use to *him*. He had better not start building bridges on the basis of any of his calculations: at least, not with his own money. Even the assurance given him, on the best authority, that he knows quite a lot would seem to be of no more use to him than the information that a majority of his answers simply happen to be right. Nor, it would seem, is the spectator's knowledge of the imaginary calculator's knowledge that the answer to the first sum is 65, of any more use to the spectator than the knowledge that the answer to the first sum is 65. To know that the answer, 65, given by the imaginary calculator is correct, might indeed be useful; but what sort of bonus is there in the further information that the imaginary calculator *knows* that the correct answer is 65?

We find, as competent speakers of English, that there are uses of the word "know" in which it is possible to know something without knowing one knows and even while falsely believing that one does not. But what might such a finding be worth? Richard Hughes, the author of *High Wind in Jamaica*, once ended a BBC broadcast talk by saying that one has forgotten what childhood is unless one remembers what it was like to go to sleep—and we quote—"knowing, really knowing, that there is a tiger under the bed." But one would surely not want to make this remark of a highly competent speaker of the English language a basis for a paper showing that one can know that *p*, even where *p* is false. One can; but knowledge of what is false is useless, insignificant, and uninteresting. Indeed, most people would not want it. And the kind of knowledge we have been talking about, which one does not know one has got or thinks one has not got, could be thought even worse. For while we can see a point to attributing the kind of knowledge of what is false to the child, the attribution of knowledge to the imaginary calculator has no point at all.

So far, we have not claimed that the attribution of such knowledge does have any point; only that it can *truly* be attributed. But while truth is essential, importance is important. Unless attribution of such knowledge has some point, our argument that it can be attributed is pretty pointless. Our bug collection will simply be ignored by the serious lepidopterist; if he is to prize one of our bugs, it must have some significance for scientific theory. If our thesis is not to bore philosophers, it must have some relevance for theory of knowledge.

One general epistemological question is "What can we properly claim to know?" The skeptic can still answer "Nothing at all," so long as our knowledge is merely that of the imaginary calculator. The epistemologist may therefore simply ignore this kind of knowledge, on the grounds that it makes no significant difference if anyone has it. He is interested only in the kind of knowledge worth having, and the knowledge of both the imaginary calculator and Richard Hughes' child is, at best, worthless. He will operate with what Hintikka calls the "philosopher's sense of the word 'know'," in which to know is to know that one knows.

We shall accept this challenge. We shall argue not only for the usefulness of the kind of knowledge we have been discussing—both that which we do not know, and that which we falsely believe is not knowledge—but also that it is absolutely essential to any dynamic and fruitful theory of knowledge. Indeed, some of it is the most valuable kind of knowledge we can have.

We begin by pointing out what more is said of the imaginary calculator in asserting that he is not merely right, but he knows. In our imaginary case, the calculator uses some, but not the same, procedure in getting each of the answers to his arithmetical problems. If there is any difference between his knowing the right answer and his merely being right, it must lie in some facts about the procedure: for only the procedure—that is, whatever he does in getting the particular answer he gets—could constitute any differences between the various cases. We must then ask: what is it about his procedure which enables us to credit him with knowledge in those cases where he is right?

We must first hasten to point out that in approaching the issue in this way, we are not making the mistake of thinking that in general the difference between knowledge and merely being right is constituted by a difference in procedure: for there are many things we know, and come to know, without going through any procedure at all. It is not our aim in this paper to set out a general theory of the difference between knowledge and true belief: there is no space for such a major undertaking, nor is it necessary for us to do so. It is sufficient if we show that knowledge acquired through some procedure may be of the kind in question, and is valuable. Accordingly, in subsequent references to theory of knowledge, we will be concerned only with that aspect of it which is concerned with knowledge acquired through some procedure.

Imagine the mathematician tells the imaginary calculator that his first answer is right, and one of the others wrong. This would not be enough for the calculator or anyone else to conclude that he knows the answer to the first question, since he could reason as follows: "Since I got one of the answers wrong, there may be something generally wrong with the way I work. It may be that the procedures I followed just happened to produce right answers to some of my questions. When I got the right answer on the first question, this may have been because while my procedure was bad, I was just lucky." What else, then, could the mathematician tell him from which he could properly conclude that he knew the first answer was right? It would surely be sufficient if the mathematician told him that the procedure he followed in finding out the first answer would always give the right answer to some independently determinable range of questions, including this one, though not of course to all questions. In the case where he got the wrong answer, he necessarily could not have used such a procedure in getting it.

It would then seem sufficient for it to be true that the calculator knows that he knows the right answer, that he knows that he got the answer by means of a procedure which would always give the right answer to a range of questions of which the problem in question is one. To attribute knowledge to the calculator is then to say considerably more than that his answer is correct: it is indeed to make a quite bold claim. It is still true, however, that unless the calculator can attribute this knowledge to himself, his knowledge is useless to him. But is it true that all such knowledge is useless to everyone? Worse, are we all in the situation of the imaginary calculator with respect to all our knowledge? Could the skeptic be right in saying that we never know that we know anything at all, though we may possess the allegedly useless kind of knowledge the imaginary calculator has?

This fear would be a real one if we could argue correctly as follows: We use many procedures to settle many different kinds of questions, and in many cases we are left in no doubt as to the answers; indeed, we confidently assert that we know them. But those of us who are reasonable and not extremely arrogant would be prepared to admit that there must be, among these many procedures, some which do not always give the right answers to the questions with which we are concerned. We must then say that some of our procedures are not sufficient for knowledge, without being able to specify which. This would appear to put us in the same position as the imaginary calculator: while there may be many things we know, we do not know that we know.

However, let us call *first order*, questions about matters other than the correctness of our procedures for answering questions, and *second order*, those about the correctness of our procedures for answering questions. Knowledge of the answers to first order questions is the first order knowledge; knowledge of the answer to second order questions, second order knowledge. Now the claim that we are in the position of the imaginary calculator with respect to all our knowledge based on procedures, amounts to saying that we have no second order knowledge. But just as we can say that the imaginary calculator has knowledge, despite the fact that in some cases his procedures lead him astray, so also we can say that it is possible for us to have second order knowledge, so long as in some cases we have right procedures for answering second order questions. And this, surely, is what we take our situation to be. We do not use all our procedures unthinkingly: we proceed to examine and criticize them. In the light of these procedures of examination and criticism, we claim to know that some of them are correct. Just so long as at least *some* of these procedures of examination and criticism are correct, some of our claims to know that we know are correct.

Which of our procedures of examination and criticism are correct is of course itself open to investigation. Such investigation may result in the rejection of some such procedures on which we had previously relied, and perhaps in the acceptance of others which we had previously regarded as unreliable. The results of such investigation will range over a variety of such putative procedures; it will give us a more comprehensive view of what may constitute first order knowledge.

The more comprehensive such a theory becomes, the more it is open to error. But it would be quite wrong to think that in the absence of a completely comprehensive theory, entirely free from error, second order knowledge is impossible. So long as our more comprehensive theories imply that some of our procedures of examination and criticism are right, which are in fact right, then we will go on correctly claiming to know that we know some of the things we know. If our comprehensive theory implies that some of our procedures of examination and criticism are right, when they are in fact unreliable, then we will falsely claim to know that we know some things which we may or may not in fact know. If our comprehensive theory implies that some of our procedures of examination and criticism are incorrect, when they are in fact correct, then it will lead us falsely to claim that we do not know that we know something which we do in fact know that we know. For which of our procedures are right ones, and hence what we know, depends not on what comprehensive theory we may hold, but on what comprehensive theory is true.

Take the following example. A man relies on an almanac for answering many different kinds of first order questions. When is the next eclipse of the moon? What is the population of Hong Kong? How far is New York from Chicago?

The question is raised whether, by using the almanac, he really knows the answers to these questions. Having so far trusted the almanac unthinkingly, the man now tries to find out whether his procedure for answering these questions is a right one. He finds out who among the astronomers are accepted as the most reliable experts, and asks them whether, with respect to astronomical information, the almanac is reliable. He is told that it is beyond reproach. He does the same for the demographical and geographical information. Surely, he now knows that his procedure for answering certain astronomical, demographical, and geographical questions, namely consulting the almanac, is a right one.

However, let us suppose the almanac also contains astrological predictions. He finds out who, among astrologers, are the acknowledged experts, and they assure him that the astrological predictions of the almanac are entirely trustworthy. He now claims to know that he knows the answers to his astrological questions are correct, and he is of course, mistaken.

He appears to have a relatively comprehensive theory about the examination and criticism of his procedures for answering first order questions. A right procedure is one which is underwritten by those who are acknowledged as experts by those who work in the relevant field. This comprehensive theory is not correct. It would apply to physics, mathematics, astronomy, and chemistry, but not to astrology, phrenology, and numerology. But this is no ground for going back on what we said before, that he knows his procedure for answering certain astronomical, demographical, and geographical questions, namely consulting the almanac, is a right one. For while his most comprehensive theory about the examination and criticism of his procedures for answering first order questions is mistaken, some of his less comprehensive ones are correct.

We are now in a position to say why the kind of knowledge in which, while we know, we do not know that we know, is the alpha and the omega of any dynamic or fruitful theory of knowledge.

It is its alpha because if a theory of knowledge is to be dynamic and fruitful, we must always allow that the limits we are tentatively inclined to draw to our knowledge are capable of modification, either by being expanded or drawn tighter. To have any second order knowledge at all is already to begin to acquire a theory of knowledge. It is probably false that we can represent ourselves as entirely without second order knowledge insofar as we know anything at all; but until our theory of knowledge is considerably developed, it is surely the case that if we have enough knowledge, enough reliable procedures to get any distance, most of that knowledge will be putative and problematic: the kind of knowledge which we do not, at that stage, know we possess. If on the other hand, all that can count as knowledge is that which we know that we have, theory of knowledge would be in a sense static. It would merely have to be brought to light, being already there, for it could not change our view of what we may know by expanding it. It could perhaps change it by restricting it, and that is why theories of knowledge traditionally seem to have been either dull and unsurprising, or interesting and sceptical.

It is its omega, because it must be the aim of theory of knowledge to develop more and more comprehensive theories of what may constitute first order knowledge. Our most comprehensive theories may or may not be correct; but in either case, our most comprehensive *correct* theories must constitute, in the absence of a more comprehensive correct theory, knowledge which we do not know we have. This may be seen in the light of the example of the man who consults the almanac. His most comprehensive theory is that those procedures are correct which are underwritten by those acknowledged as experts by those working in the field. This comprehensive theory is mistaken; for it implies that a correct procedure for answering astrological questions is to look them up in the almanac. However, it implies a less comprehensive theory which is, anyway, roughly correct: that those procedures for answering scientific questions are correct which are underwritten by those acknowledged as experts by those working in the field. Because of this, it is true of him that he knows of his procedures for finding out the answers to scientific questions that they are correct. But he does not know that he knows this.

We can also explain why some knowledge of the kind we have discussed—knowledge which we do not know we have—is the most valuable kind of knowledge we have. We have said that what someone knows depends on what comprehensive theories of second order knowledge are true, not on what comprehensive theories he may happen to hold. So acquiring a relatively comprehensive theory does not make any difference to the first order knowledge one already has. But, much more important, it is likely to *increase* our first order knowledge. Knowing which are some of the right procedures, and which some of the wrong, enables us to concentrate on the former rather than the latter, and thus increase our first order knowledge. Having highly comprehensive and correct theories of knowledge enables us to increase such second order knowledge, and hence to multiply our first order knowledge. The most comprehensive theories of second order knowledge we possess must therefore be the most valuable kind we can have. But, as we have seen already, our most comprehensive correct theories of knowledge themselves involve the kind of knowledge we have been discussing: knowledge which we cannot be said to know that we have. Such knowledge is, indeed, so valuable, that we should always seek it, even though we can never say we have finally found it.

Those epistomologists who would deny the possibility of the kind of knowledge we have been discussing tend towards two opposite kinds of dogmatism. They tend either to a denial of the principle of gullibility, with the result that one must search for some incorrigible starting points to knowledge, some basic propositions beyond question; or to wholesale skepticism, in which the whole of human knowledge is completely swept away. Our position is more modest than either of these. There is much we would claim to know, but we keep open the possibility of revision; on the other hand, there is much that we would claim not to know, but we hold open the possibility of amendment there, too. Such revision, such amendment, is a part of intellectual progress. We cherish our modesty, not just because it is charming, but because we believe it to be fruitful.

University of Wisconsin AND
University of Warwick

Emotions and Belief
O. H. GREEN

BELIEFS of certain sorts are characteristic of the several emotions.[1] A belief that one has suffered some loss is characteristic of grief, for example, and a belief that one is in some danger is characteristic of fear. This much is generally recognized. But there are several questions about the relationship between emotions and belief as yet unresolved in philosophical discussion. (1) Can the concept of the object of an emotion be explained in terms of beliefs? (2) Are characteristic beliefs logically involved in having an emotion? (3) Are beliefs of certain kinds causes of emotions? (4) How do beliefs figure in the justification of emotions? In this essay answers to these questions will be attempted.

I. What Is the Object of an Emotion?

The relationship between belief and emotions has been perhaps most frequently considered in connection with discussions of objects of emotion. The concept of the object of an emotion is, of course, an important one and has come in for a good deal of discussion, but it remains very much in need of a satisfactory analysis. A large part of this paper will be concerned with the elucidation of this concept. This analysis will involve examining some familiar approaches to determining what the object of a person's emotion is, in order to see whether any of them provides a sound basis for understanding the concept of the object of an emotion.

Several ways of finding out what the object of a person's emotion is are commonly employed in everyday life. (1) In order to tell what the object of a person's anger, fear, or embarrassment is, we may consider what he is inclined to attack, avoid, or cover up. The object of a person's emotion would appear to be indicated by characteristic patterns in his action and desire. (2) We may inquire what a person takes to be provocative, what wrong he thinks he has done, or what

---

[1] Application of the term "emotion" is throughout restricted to a range of conative-affective states including embarrassment, pity, grief, indignation, fear, remorse, and other quite similar examples.

loss he believes he has suffered in order to discover the object of his anger, remorse, or grief. Certain sorts of beliefs are supposed, roughly, to be about the object of the emotion. (3) Another way of ascertaining the object of a person's emotion is suggested by Anthony Kenny in *Action, Emotion and Will*. It is explained as follows:

> Faced with any sentence describing the occurrence of an emotion, of the form "*A* φd because *p*," we must ask whether it is a necessary condition of the truth of this sentence that *A* should know or believe that *p*. If so, then the sentence contains an allusion to the object of the emotion; if not, to its cause.[2]

Like the ways of determining the object of a person's emotion already considered, this approach is often used in everyday life when we ask why a person is grieved, indignant, or jealous and take the answer to indicate the object of the emotion in question. Kenny's account is designed to point out that not just any answer is taken to indicate the object, but only one which satisfies certain conditions. (4) In order to learn what the object of a person's embarrassment, gratitude, love, pity, or hate is, we may ask what he is embarrassed about, afraid of, or grateful to, or what he loves, pities, or hates. It seems that in a sentence describing a person's emotion the object of the emotion is indicated by the grammatical object of the appropriate preposition or verb.

Of these familiar ways of determining what the object of a person's emotion is, only (2) and (3) explicitly involve a consideration of beliefs. Each of the four ways appears to provide a plausible suggestion for analyzing the concept of the object of an emotion, however, and these suggestions must be considered.

II. Behavior and Objects of Emotion

Let us first consider whether the object of a person's emotion is indicated by his tendencies to engage in certain characteristic patterns of action. It is surely beyond doubt that we are often able to tell what the object of a person's emotion is by considering his behavior.

There are, however, questions which may be raised about the efficacy of the consideration of behavior in determining the object of a person's emotion. Purposive behavior characteristic of an emotion is most likely to provide an indication of what the object of a person's emotion is. A person's covering something up, for example, is likely to indicate what he is embarrassed about if any behavior will. But no sort of purposive behavior is characteristic of

[2] London, 1963, p. 75.

C

some emotions. Grief, despair, sorrow, and depressive emotions generally are examples. And even where some form of purposive behavior is characteristic of an emotion, a person who experiences the emotion may, for some reason, fail to behave in the appropriate way. Thus, a person who is angry with another may refrain from any kind of attack for fear of the consequences, and a person who is remorseful may not attempt any sort of reparation because he thinks it would do no good. In these cases, which are numerous, behavior is unlikely to provide any indication of the object of a person's emotion. We are not, on that account, always unable to say what the object of a person's emotion is in such cases, however. This suggests that an explanation of the concept of the object of an emotion in terms of characteristic behavior would be inadequate.

There is, however, a more fundamental objection to analyzing the concept of the object of an emotion in terms of behavior. Probably characteristic forms of purposive behavior appear promising as indicators of the object of a person's emotion because action of this type takes an object. The object of an action is often what is acted on. In such cases, however, the object of an action is, unlike the object of an emotion, not an intentional object. It is, of course, difficult to set out necessary and sufficient conditions for an object's being an intentional object, but the following will suffice for present purposes as a mark of intentionality. If a name or description indicates or specifies an intentional object, then a simple declarative sentence in which it occurs neither implies that there is, nor that there is not, something to which it applies. On this criterion it is clear that objects of emotion are intentional and that objects of action, where the object is what is acted on, are not. It could be true that A assaulted B only if there was someone who was assaulted by A, for example, but it could be true that A feared evil spirits whether or not any existed. The fact that emotions are intentional in this way, while actions usually are not, is sufficient to preclude the possibility of analyzing the concept of the object of an emotion by identifying objects of emotion with objects of actions of the relevant sort.

The object of an emotion may on occasion be the same thing as the object of the characteristic behavior which it involves, but there will be many cases where this is not so, at least where the emotion involves no actual behavior and where the intentional object of the emotion does not exist. There is thus an insurmountable barrier to analyzing the concept of the object of an emotion in terms of behavior. An appeal to wishes and desires for the relevant type of behavior however, avoids the difficulties involved in a behavioral analysis.

Although a person who has an emotion may fail to engage in purposive behavior characteristic of the emotion, either because no purposive behavior is characteristic of the emotion or because of some reason particular to the case, it is reasonable to suppose that the person must nonetheless have some desire or wish for some form of action relevant to the emotion which he has. Thus, a person who is angry but refrains from attack for fear of the consequences presumably still wants to attack, and a person who feels remorse but attempts no reparation because he thinks it would do no good no doubt still wishes he could do something to put right what he has done. Even a person who is grieved by an irretrievable loss still wishes he could recover what he has lost. While objects of action usually are not intentional, objects of desire, like objects of emotion, are intentional objects. It may be true that a person wants to ø whether or not he does so.

It is clear on reflection, however, that the object of an emotion is not the same as the object of a desire or wish which it involves. For example, where a man is insulted by another and wants to hit him, what he wants is to hit the man, but the object of his anger is clearly the man who insulted him.

There is a basic difficulty which applies to attempts to give an account of objects of emotion both in terms of characteristic purposive behavior and in terms of wishes or desires for such behavior. In order to appreciate this difficulty it is necessary to recall that a person's behavior and desires for the same sort of behavior count as emotional only when occurring in circumstances taken in a certain way.[3] Where a person's behavior is clearly emotional, we can say that he behaved as he did because he believed the circumstances to be of a certain kind. For example, a man's hurriedly leaving the country can well be taken to be frightened avoidance of something he believes to be in some way dangerous, and a man's attack on another can only be taken as an act of jealousy if he believes that the man he sets upon is his wife's lover or something of the sort. This being the case, it would seem that any attempt to explain the concept of the object of an emotion in terms of characteristic patterns of action or desire would, in effect, be based on, or would involve, an account of the same notion in terms of the appropriate beliefs. Thus, a purely behavioral account of objects of emotion would, at the very least, be incomplete or misleading.

[3] For a more detailed presentation of this idea see my article "The Expression of Emotion," *Mind*, vol. 79 (1970), pp. 551–568.

III. BELIEFS AND OBJECTS OF EMOTION

Beliefs which are characteristic of the several emotions provide a promising basis for giving an account of objects of emotion. Of course, if the intentionality of emotions is to be explained in terms of such beliefs, they must be generally involved in having an emotion. At the outset it must be insisted that the notion of belief not be taken too narrowly here. It may be more natural in many cases to speak of seeing, thinking, assuming, knowing, feeling, suspecting, or taking it that such-and-such rather than of believing that such-and-such. For this reason, if we are to speak of belief in this context, the notion must be construed quite broadly. Having said this, however, it seems clear that characteristic beliefs are logically involved in having an emotion. If a man does not believe that another has suffered some undeserved misfortune, he cannot feel pity for him, for instance, and if a man does not believe that he has suffered some loss, he cannot feel grief.

It might be argued, however, that even so, characteristic beliefs are not conceptually involved in having the several emotions. It seems, for example, that a belief that one is in some danger is not conceptually involved in being afraid since there appear to be cases in which something is feared although no danger is anticipated. There might be a man who is afraid of mice or clouds even though he does not believe that they will do actual harm. He pales and trembles at the sight of clouds or mice, he says timorously that mice or clouds are horrible things, and he takes cover when clouds appear or has the pest control service visit his home daily. But he tells us, for example, that he does not believe that mice bite, carry diseases, or destroy property, or that clouds bring damaging rains and lightning.

This man's fear is irrational; we might call it a phobia. His behavior is incongruous with his denials that he has the appropriate beliefs. This point is important. It is only because his behavior is appropriate to the anticipation of danger that we say that he is afraid, in view of his denials that he believes some harm to be imminent. If there were no evidence of some anticipation of danger, the concept of fear would gain no foothold. Thus, if a case were produced where it was quite clear that no anticipation of danger existed, it would be a case which was not clearly an example of fear.

It might be thought that cases in which emotions are "objectless" present a difficulty for the view that characteristic beliefs are logically connected with emotions. This does not seem to be the case, however. If a person who is afraid, but has no idea what he is afraid of, believes himself to be in some indeterminate danger, his emotion will be irrational by way of being based on a belief incapable of substantiation; the case presents no difficulty for the view under consideration since a characteristic belief is present. If such a person denies that he believes it to be so that he is in any danger, but behaves as though he did, his emotion will also be irrational by way of being incongruous with his profession of disbelief; but since there is still evidence of characteristic belief, this case too can be accommodated. If there is no evidence that such a person believes himself in any danger, however, there is also no evidence that he is afraid.

Although some doubts may arise about whether having an emotion necessarily involves certain kinds of beliefs, it seems that these doubts can be resolved. Where a person has an emotion and a belief of the sort characteristic of that emotion, we can say of him that he has the emotion because he believes that such-and-such, or where it is understood that the person's believing that p is a necessary condition of the truth of the description given of his emotion, that he has the emotion because p. This is, of course, the form of description which is required for Kenny's test for determining what the object of a person's emotion is. We can thus, in discussing the efficacy of characteristic beliefs, consider whether Kenny's test enables us to tell what the object of a person's emotion is.

Some emotions often take persons or groups of persons as objects. With such emotions Kenny's test will not serve unamended to determine the object of the emotion. Anger and gratitude are examples of the emotions which take persons as objects. Descriptions of the occurrence of these emotions may be of the form Kenny's test requires: "Billy was angry because his knuckles were rapped," or "He was grateful because he had been so honored." In such cases it is a necessary condition of the truth of the description that the person believe that his knuckles had been rapped or that he had been so honored. But allusion or reference to the object of his anger or gratitude is not made since the "because"-clause is in the passive mood and therefore no mention of the agent is made. With agent- or person-directed emotions like anger and gratitude, mention of the agent is crucial. A straightforward amendment is sufficient to take care of this difficulty, however. It seems fair to say that a description of an action is incomplete if it does not include a reference to the agent. If this is agreed, we can require that where a person's emotion is said to be due to a belief about an action, the description of the action must be complete in this respect. Mention of the object of agent-directed emotions in the "because"-clause will thus be assured.

There are many cases in which a difficulty arises for the kind of test which Kenny proposes that is not easily resolved. In these cases Kenny's test fails to provide us with any basis for saying what the object of a person's emotion is because it gives only an ambiguous indication of the object. Examples are descriptions of the occurrence of person-directed emotions completed to include reference to the agent in the "because"-clause. "She was afraid because the bear was getting closer to her hiding place" is also a case in point. Here reference is made to the bear, which is, of course, the object of her fear; but reference is also made to her hiding place, although she is presumably not afraid of her hiding place. Kenny's test does not enable us to decide which referent is the object of her fear.

Difficulties about the ambiguity of indication could be avoided, perhaps, if objects of emotion were identified with objects of the belief expressed in the "because"-clause. The object of A's emotion described in "A ød that (or because) p" would always be specified propositionally by p. But objects of emotion are often taken to be non-propositional—where Red Riding Hood is afraid of the Big Bad Wolf, for example. More significantly, there are a number of emotions which do not take propositional objects. Pity, hate, love, and resentment are examples. A person cannot be said to pity, love, hate, resent (etc.) that or because p. There appears to be a feature of these emotions which explains this grammatical fact. What is pitied, hated, loved, or resented must, respectively, be believed to suffer undeserved misfortune, to be evil, to be attractive, or to have been slighting or injurious. But states of affairs are indicated by propositional clauses, and states of affairs are not the right sort of thing to be the subject of such beliefs. A propositional account of objects of emotion generally is unacceptable. Kenny apparently does not take a propositional view of objects of emotion, however. He says that

> . . . the sense of "object" which I have . . . employed . . . is one which derives from the grammatical notion of the object of a transitive verb. The object of fear is what is feared, the object of love is what is loved . . . .[4]

IV. The Grammatical Criterion

According to the grammatical criterion, as it is commonly construed, the object of an emotion is indicated by the grammatical object of the appropriate verb or preposition in a sentence describing

[4] *Op. cit.*, pp. 187–188.

ı person's emotion. The sentence will be one like "Abelard loved Heloise" or "Othello is jealous of Cassio." That is, the description will be such that an emotion is attributed to a person, and the emotion word takes a grammatical object, either with or without a preposition.

In an article called "Emotion and Object," J. C. Gosling argues that the grammatical criterion is virtually worthless:

> Verbalization fails to help us simply because in the last resort it relies on nothing stronger than the force of idiom. In the last resort idiom is either indecisive or lacking, and then some other criterion is required.[5]

It is important to see whether Gosling is right, particularly in view of the difficulties in explaining the concept of the object of an emotion in terms of emotional behavior or beliefs.

As was pointed out, on the usual understanding of the grammatical criterion, the object of an emotion is indicated by the grammatical object of the appropriate verb or preposition. Gosling thinks that prepositions are no help in understanding what the object of a person's emotion is because:

> There are a number of emotions which characteristically take two prepositions in the required way: gratitude has to be *to* a benefactor *for* a benefit, anger *with* someone *about* something, and so on. . . . So we have the question whether in these cases we have two objects.[6]

Verbs are no more useful than prepositions in determining the object of a person's emotion, according to Gosling. Not every emotion word has a verb form which takes an object without a preposition which could be used in describing a person's emotion, and there is no reason to prefer artificial forms which do.[7]

It is possible to make some headway in remedying these defects in the grammatical criterion pointed out by Gosling. It is true that "anger," for example, takes more than one preposition. But when a person has been struck by another and is angry, can we indiscriminately say that he was angry with or about the person or the blow? Of course not. We would say that he is angry with the person about the blow. Or, alternatively, we might say that he was angry with the man because the man struck him. Our use of prepositions with emotion verbs, where there may be two, is not arbitrary. The fact that double preposition descriptions like the one considered can be recast as suggested hints at a reason for this. The alternative descrip-

---

[5] *The Philosophical Review*, vol. 74 (1965), p. 488.
[6] *Ibid.*
[7] *Ibid.*

tion is of the form "*A* ød *x* because *p*"; in descriptions of this form, ø is replaceable by an emotion verb or emotion phrase, with or without a preposition, and *p* is a propositional clause setting out a belief which *A* must have if the description is to be true. In a later section of this paper, it will be argued that thoughts characteristic of emotion are their causes or occasions and that occasions of emotion are different from objects of emotion. A person's thought that another struck him may occasion his anger, but the object of his anger is not his thought that the other person struck him; it would seem to be the person who struck him. Propositional clauses which replace *p* in descriptions of the form "*A* ød *x* because *p*" generally express the thought which occasions *A*'s emotion. This suggests that when we say that the man was angry with the other about the blow, the object of the anger is specified by the grammatical object of "with," while the content of the thought which is the occasion of the anger is indicated by the grammatical object of "about." And this suggestion might be generalized, so that we can say that, in cases like that of "anger," where there may be more than one preposition, the object of the emotion is indicated by the prepositional object which does not specify the content of the thought which is the occasion of the emotion.

If this suggestion is acceptable, it will, in effect, take care of Gosling's objections. For where there is not a form of emotion verb which takes an object without a preposition, there seems always to be one which takes a preposition and object. If prepositions are vindicated from the charges made by Gosling, there is no reason why we cannot use them to supplement verbs in determining the object of an emotion.

This defense of the grammatical criterion, however, makes no more than a little headway. It is true that our use of prepositions in describing emotions is not arbitrary. It may even be true that the object of an emotion is indicated by the grammatical object of the preposition in such descriptions as "He was angry with the man because the man struck him," but this has not been shown. Where we can say "He was angry with the man because the man struck him," we can also say "He was angry that the man struck him." If we take the grammatical object of the preposition in the first description to indicate the object of the man's anger, the object would be the man who struck him. But in the second description, the object of his emotion seems to be specified by the propositional clause, and in that case would be the fact that the man struck him. An appeal to the distinction between objects and occasions of emotion does nothing to clarify matters. The problem of ambiguous or indecisive indication of the object of an emotion remains in the grammatical criterion, as Gosling suspects, but it comes out basically in a different way from that which he suggests.

Generally speaking, the problem here is that in descriptions of emotions, objects of emotion can often alternatively be specified non-propositionally, by x in a description of the form "A ød x because p," or propositionally, by p in descriptions of the form "A ød that p"; and the objects indicated in these two ways will not be the same. Any choice to take the propositional or the non-propositional specification of the object would, without further reason, be arbitrary. Because of this, the grammatical criterion unaided fails to give any general guide to a clear determination of objects of emotion.

V. A Theory of Objects of Emotion

There are difficulties in the way of giving an account of the concept of the object of an emotion based on desire or belief, and a satisfactory analysis of the concept in terms of grammatical considerations seems out of the question. Still, there is something puzzling about this state of affairs. Of the components of an emotion, so to speak, desire and belief are the only ones which are intentional in their own right, and it is often by considering belief and desire that we learn what the object of a person's emotion is. It is thus a bit odd that the concept of the object of an emotion should not be derivative from that of the object of desires and beliefs characteristic of emotions, and that neither desire nor belief should figure in a generally satisfactory approach to determining what the object of an emotion is.

A suggestion seems to be in order which would give desire and belief the place they appear to deserve in the explanation of the intentionality of emotion. The suggestion is, roughly, that the object of an emotion is what the objects of the characteristic desire and belief involved in having the emotion have in common. More precisely put, it is that the object of an emotion is what is mentioned in a complete specification of the objects of both the characteristic belief and desire which it involves. The clarity and plausibility of this suggestion may be enhanced by the consideration of some examples. (1) A is angry with B because B insulted him. B can be seen to be the object of A's anger from a look at the desire and belief characteristic of anger which A has. That B insulted A is the object of the relevant belief. And, if we suppose that *A* wants to hit *B*, hitting *B* is the object of the appropriate desire. Since *B* is mentioned in the specification of the objects of *A*'s belief and desire characteristic of anger, *B* is the object of his emotion. (2) *A* is afraid that he will lose his job. That *A* will lose his job is the object of *A*'s belief characteristic of fear. And, if *A* wants to avoid losing his job, the avoidance of the loss of his job is the object of *A*'s desire characteristic of fear. That *A* will lose his job is indicated as the object of *A*'s fear, in view of the fact that this is what is mentioned in the specification of the objects of the relevant desire and belief.

If the suggestion illustrated in these examples is accepted, it seems to resolve the puzzle about the intentionality of emotion. The notion of the object of an emotion will, in a way, be derivative from that of the objects of desires and beliefs characteristic of emotions, and it will be possible to ascertain what the object of a person's emotion is by considering the relevant desires and beliefs he has.

The approach to discovering the object of a person's emotion implicit in the suggestion that the concept can be understood in terms of desires and beliefs of the appropriate sorts, is not subject to the difficulties which attend the consideration of desires or beliefs alone. Where the object of an emotion is not the propositional object of the appropriate belief, this will be made clear by the consideration of the object of the relevant desire. Thus, that his boss looks down on him is not the object of Fred's hatred where he hates his boss because he has a belief with this object, but considering that it is his boss he wants to get at makes this clear. Of course, getting at his boss is not the object of Fred's hatred, either, as a consideration of his relevant belief makes clear. The fact that objects of emotion are not the same as objects of desire is pointed up by taking into account the object of the belief.

There are some counter-examples to the thesis that the object of an emotion is what is mentioned in a complete specification of the objects of the characteristic belief and desire which it involves. Consider the following cases. (1) *A* is angry with *B* because *B* has been reading his private diary. That *B* has been reading his diary is the object of *A*'s belief characteristic of anger. If *A* wants to throw the diary at *B*, throwing the book at *B* is the object of the relevant desire. But since both *B* and the book are mentioned in the specification of the objects of the appropriate belief and desire, we are given an ambiguous indication of the object of *A*'s anger. (2) *A* feels remorse about breaking the promise he made. That *A* broke his promise is the object of his belief characteristic of remorse. If we suppose that

A wants to keep all future promises, keeping all promises in the future is the object of the relevant desire.[8] But, since reference is not made in the specification of the objects of the appropriate desire and belief to a single thing, we are given no clear indication of the object of *A*'s remorse.

There is a fact about the relation between beliefs and desires characteristic of an emotion and involved in its occurrence which seems to enable us to deal with counter-examples like these. The beliefs in question provide a reason for having the relevant desires. In the case of pity, for example, my belief that a man has suffered some undeserved misfortune provides a reason for my desire to help him. If we bear in mind this relation between beliefs and desires characteristically involved in having an emotion, we can see that *B* is the object of *A*'s anger, and that breaking a promise he made is the object of *A*'s remorse in the above examples. For where *A* is angry with *B* because *B* has been reading his private diary, *A*'s belief will provide a reason for desiring only those actions characteristic of anger which have to do with *B*. And if *A* feels remorse about breaking a promise he made, *A*'s belief that he broke a promise will only provide him with a reason for desiring to do something characteristic of remorse related to breaking the promise.

The present suggestion about objects of emotion can be applied in remedying the indecisiveness of the grammatical criterion. Thus, we find that sometimes emotional objects are indicated by *p* in "*A* øative d that *p*," but otherwise by *x* in "*A* ød *x* because *p*." This reflects the facts that the object of an emotion is sometimes the object of the relevant belief, that it is not the same as the object of the appropriate desire, but that it is mentioned in any case in the complete specifications of the objects of both, provided that the belief gives a reason for having the desire.

VI. Occasions of Emotion

The occasion of a person's emotion is a proximate cause of the emotion within his field of consciousness. A person's experiences remote in time from the occurrence of the emotion, and his physiological state of which he is not aware, may both be causes of his emotions, but they cannot occasion them. It will be argued that

[8] Of course, we might suppose instead that *A* wants to make reparation for breaking his promise, in which case there is no problem. But the desire to mend one's ways, and not just to make amends, is characteristic of remorse.

occasions of emotions are thoughts of a certain kind characteristic of the emotion in question and that they are distinct from objects of emotion.

Consider the following cases:

(1) Robert is embarrassed because he is late for the dinner party.
(2) Robert is embarrassed because he thinks that he is late for the dinner party, but in fact he is not late.

It should be noted that the belief which Robert has in these cases is characteristic of the emotion attributed to him. Embarrassment characteristically involves the belief that one's actions, appearance, or possessions, or those of a person felt to be connected in some way with oneself, will be found unseemly.

In the second case we are inclined to say that it is Robert's thought which is the occasion of his emotion. If Robert is not late, his lateness cannot be the cause of his embarrassment. But if he had not thought that he was late, Robert would not have been embarrassed. Our inclination to say that a thought is the occasion of an emotion is reinforced in this and in other cases by additional considerations. If Robert is embarrassed because he thinks that he is late and is persuaded that he is not late, his embarrassment will presumably disappear. And even where Robert was late, the mere thought of his tardiness may long after cause Robert to feel embarrassed. The suggestion that it is a thought which is the occasion of the emotion in the first case is likely to be resisted, however. If Robert was late, his tardiness would seem to be the cause of his embarrassment.

It is strange somehow to say that sometimes the occasion of an emotion is a thought and sometimes not—that, for example, where Robert is correct in thinking that he is late, it is his lateness which is the occasion of his embarrassment; but where he is mistaken in thinking this, it is his thought which is the cause of his emotion. Clearly, where Robert only thinks that he is late, his tardiness cannot be the cause of his embarrassment; there is no possibility of saying that it is always some unseemly action or appearance which is the occasion of a person's embarrassment. Can we then assimilate all cases to those in which the occasion of an emotion is clearly a thought? This seems to be the most plausible step to take.

In the case where Robert is late and is embarrassed, he would presumably not have been embarrassed if he had not been late. But still Robert must have believed that he was late; for even if he was late, if Robert did not think that he was late, he would not have been embarrassed. Thus, we can, even in cases like this one, say that thoughts characteristic of the emotion are the occasions of the emotion.

It seems clear that a person may sometimes have a belief of the sort characteristic of an emotion without its giving rise to the emotion. For example, even a dedicated campaigner for equal rights in housing may fail to feel indignation when, on reading the morning paper, he comes to believe that black families are being kept out of the new housing estate; he may be too tired or too busy to care, at least for the moment. Beliefs which are the occasions of emotions are not sufficient empirical conditions for their occurrence. They do seem to be necessary empirical conditions for the occurrence of emotions, however. Indeed, it has been argued that where there is no evidence of such a belief, there is no reason to suppose that there is an emotion. But this very fact may give rise to doubts about the claim that characteristic beliefs are causes of emotions.

Before objections are considered, however, it remains to show that objects of emotion are not occasions of emotion. To do this we may consider the ways in which the object of an emotion may be indicated. Where we have a description of an emotion of the form "*A* øds *x* because *p*," the object of the emotion may be non-propositionally indicated by *x*, while the thought which is the occasion of the emotion is expressed in the "because"-clause. In such cases, object and occasion are clearly distinct. Where we have descriptions of emotions of the form "*A* ød that *p*," the "that"-clause may both propositionally specify the object of the emotion and set out the thought which is its occasion. This does not mean that in such cases object and occasion are the same, however. If an M.P. is indignant that his bill was not passed, it is his thought that his bill was not passed which is the occasion of his emotion; but he is indignant, not that he thinks that his bill was not passed, but that the bill was not passed.

Now some objections to the view that thoughts characteristic of emotions are causes or occasions of emotions must be discussed. It has been argued that when a person says, for instance, that he is angry because he was insulted, he cannot be making a causal statement, because his statement is neither based on evidence nor open to mistake.[9] Now, such considerations have a bearing on whether the statement is a causal statement only insofar as they tend to show that the statement cannot be taken to be false in the light of parallel

[9] This line of argument was used, for example, in B. A. O. Williams' "Pleasure and Belief," *Proceedings of the Aristotelian Society, Supplementary Volume,* vol. 33 (1959), pp. 57–73.

negative instances. In fact, these considerations have little importance for our purposes, interesting as they are. Whether or not such statements are based on evidence, and whether or not a person can be mistaken in making them, it is possible that a statement of this kind should be taken to be false in virtue of parallel negative instances. Suppose, for example, that the person who says that he is angry because he was insulted is a politician known for remaining cool and unruffled in the face of jibes and insults, and, moreover, that the insult came from a man who was making a play for his wife. In such a case, we might well say that it was not his belief that he had been insulted, but his belief that the man was making advances to his wife, which occasioned his anger.

In "Emotion and Thought," Irving Thalberg argues that thoughts cannot be causes of emotions. His argument consists in an application of the following principle to the case of emotions: "Anytime you claim that one event or consideration is a cause of another event or consideration, you must be able to gather evidence of the effect which is logically independent of your evidence of its putative cause."[10] The resultant argument, in a generalized form, might be put this way. To show that a person has an emotion is to show that he has a belief which is characteristic of the emotion in question, and for this reason the principle of logical independence is violated in saying that characteristic beliefs cause emotions. The argument, however, is unconvincing. The principle on which it rests, that logical connection precludes causal connection, is either false or misapplied. Thalberg and many others have overlooked the fact that many descriptions are applicable only where a certain causal relation is supposed to hold. The causal relation is built into the meaning of such descriptions. Where this is the case, the fact that a logical connection obtains will not preclude the existence of a causal connection. For example, a burn is by definition an injury caused by contact with heat; thus, where there is a burn, of course there is contact with heat, but this hardly means that contact with heat is not the cause of the burn. The case of emotion words is similar: a given emotion word can be partially defined as an affective state caused by a thought of a certain sort. "Fear," for example, is an emotion word which can be partially defined as an affective state caused by the anticipation of some danger. This being the case, there is no reason to suppose that the logical relation between emotions and thoughts precludes a causal connection.

[10] *American Philosophical Quarterly*, vol. 1 (1964), pp. 45–55; reprinted in *The Philosophy of Mind*, ed. Stuart Hampshire (New York, 1966), pp. 215 ff.

The analogy between the case of burns and heat, where the causal connection is admitted, and that of emotions and beliefs might be contested, however. Where there is a burn there is tissue damage of a certain sort which can be identified independently of the contact with heat which is its cause. But it might be thought that where there is an emotion, there is nothing corresponding to the tissue damage which can be identified independently of the belief which is supposed to be its cause. The suggestion that behavior and sensations of certain sorts in the case of emotions correspond to the tissue damage in the case of burns seems a plausible one here, but it might be rejected because emotional behavior and feelings of emotion can be identified as such only by reference to the appropriate beliefs. The suggestion should not be rejected, however, for the analogy holds. Tissue damage cannot be identified as a burn without reference to heat.

VII. Beliefs and the Justification of Emotion

Arguments similar to the one just considered have frequently been used in recent discussions of action. It is urged, for example, that desires are reasons for actions, not their causes, because there are logical connections between action and desire. One difficulty, aside from that of whether the logical connections which obtain preclude the existence of a causal connection, is present in any such argument. It is not enough to show that a belief is a reason for an emotion, for example, to show that it is, or is not, a cause of the emotion. What more is required for a belief to be a reason for an emotion?

In order to be a reason for an emotion, a belief must explain the emotion. It must be possible to say that a person has the emotion because he has the belief, and to offer the fact that he has the belief as an answer to the question of why he feels the emotion. But this does not serve to set off reasons from causes, or from causes which are not reasons. Something more is required. A promising step toward explaining what is needed is this: where a belief provides a reason for an emotion, it is possible to assess the emotion as rational or irrational, reasonable or unreasonable, justified or unjustified at least in part by reference to the belief. If the belief is rational, reasonable, or justified, then all other things being equal, the emotion will be rational, reasonable, or justified; if the belief is one which is irrational, unreasonable, or unjustified, then the emotion will be unjustified, unreasonable, or irrational. This step does enable us to separate reasons from causes which are not reasons.

Beliefs characteristic of the several emotions do, in fact, provide reasons for them in this way, in addition to being their causes or occasions. Although a person's fear or grief may be unreasonable or unjustified (even though his belief that he is in some danger or has suffered some loss is reasonable and justified) because, for instance, he goes to extremes in his emotion, it is clear that if his belief is unreasonable or unjustified, his emotion will be so as well.

Four major questions about emotions and belief have been discussed in this essay, and in conclusion the answers arrived at may be briefly reviewed. (1) The concept of the object of an emotion cannot be explained in terms of beliefs alone, but beliefs together with desires do figure in a plausible explanation. (2) Characteristic beliefs are logically involved in having an emotion. (3) Beliefs of certain kinds are causes or occasions of emotions. (4) Beliefs provide reasons for emotion and are thus essential to the justification of emotion.[11]

Tulane University

[11] I am indebted to Dr. Anthony Kenny and Professor Bernard Williams for comments on an earlier version of this article.

Descartes on Other Minds
DONALD F. HENZE

I

EVEN the beginner in philosophy is likely to know the plot of the *Meditations:* the methodical doubt is applied universally, its relentless spread halted at last by the *cogito*; then God's existence is demonstrated—twice for good measure—and thereby (so it has seemed to many readers) the principle that clear and distinct ideas are true is justified; finally it is proved that material things exist and that Descartes' mind—the "thinking thing" of the *cogito*—is utterly distinct from his body. In sum, Descartes thinks he has proved the existence of a finite, created, thinking, and unextended substance (himself); an infinite, uncreated, supremely perfect substance (God); and an indefinitely large number of finite, created, extended, and non-thinking substances (bodies).

Questions of validity and soundness aside, these are surely heroic endeavors, and the third one—the attempted proof of an external world—may even provoke a sympathetic response from some modern metaphysicians. Yet the sophisticated modern reader may be struck also by the *absence*, in the *Meditations*, of a task that has become a stock effort in contemporary philosophizing: arguing for, or justifying belief in, the existence of other (human) minds. It is curious that in the *Meditations* Descartes does not apply himself with dispatch to this job; nor does he in the *Principles*, the *Discourse*, or elsewhere. To regard this omission as a curiosity is not, I think, merely a projection of our own metaphysical concerns, for one of Descartes' chief announced aims in the *Meditations* is to prove that the human soul, or mind, is immortal, and presumably he is not thinking only of *his* own soul or of a class of hypothetical human souls.[1] Moreover Descartes is much taxed to explain the relation of mind to body, and again, presumably, his worry is not limited to

[1] Cf. this remark in the Synopsis of the *Meditations:* ". . . what I have said is sufficient to show clearly enough that the extinction of the mind does not follow from the corruption of the body, and also to give men the hope of another life after death . . . .' *The Philosophical Works of Descartes*, tr. by E. S. Haldane and G. R. T. Ross (Cambridge, 1931; as republished in New York, 1955), vol. 1, p. 141.

just *his* mind and body. And in the opening paragraph of Section V of the *Discourse*, Descartes, having proved "the existence of God and the soul," ventures to say that he has "not only found a way to satisfy myself about the principal problems that are usually dealt with in philosophy, but also discerned certain laws that God has established in nature, and of which he has implanted *ideas in our minds*, such that *on sufficient reflection we cannot doubt* that they are exactly observed by all objects and events in the world" [italics added].[2] So, it would appear that measured by his own interests, Descartes' overall strategy lacks complete symmetry between categories of substance and arguments that are supposed to prove that there are instances of such substances.

This lacuna has been noted briefly by at least one commentator, F. C. Copleston, although his suggestion for filling the gap on Descartes' behalf seems to me mistaken or at least misleading. I quote in full the relevant paragraph from his *History of Philosophy*:

> Descartes deals rather summarily with the existence of bodies. Moreover, neither in the *Meditations* nor in the *Principles of Philosophy* does he treat specifically the problem of our knowledge of the existence of other minds. But his general argument is that we receive impressions and "ideas" and that as God has implanted in us a natural inclination to attribute them to the activity of external material causes, the latter must exist. For God would be a deceiver, were He to give us this natural inclination and yet at the same time to produce these impressions directly and immediately by His own activity. And Descartes, if called upon, would doubtless produce an analogous argument, with an appeal to the divine veracity, to existence, the existence of other minds.[3]

Professor Gilbert Ryle is closer to the truth when he says, in the opening chapter of *The Concept of Mind*, that according to "Descartes' myth,"

> . . . one person has no direct access of any sort to the events of the inner life of another. He cannot do better than make problematic inferences from the observed behavior of the other person's body to the states of mind which, by analogy from his own conduct, he supposes to be signalized by that behaviour.[4]

But of course Ryle's concern with Cartesian dualism is not historical to any great extent, so the textual backing for his suggestion, as it applies to Descartes himself, is lacking.

[2] *Descartes: Philosophical Writings*, tr. and ed. by Elizabeth Anscombe and Peter Thomas Geach (London, 1954), p. 38.

[3] *A History of Philosophy*, Vol. IV: *Modern Philosophy: Descartes to Leibniz* (Garden City, New York, 1963), chap. 4, Sect. 1, p. 126.

[4] London, 1949, p. 14. Cf. Strawson's discussion of the "Cartesian view," *Individuals* (London, 1959), chap. III, Sects. 3 and 4.

What I want to do in this paper is to supply some evidence for the view that Descartes' thinking about the existence of other finite, created, thinking, and unextended substances—in short, other human minds—takes the form, approximately, of argument by analogy. In doing this I shall be commenting on the inadequacy of Copleston's suggestion that the Cartesian argument for other minds would be similar to the argument, resting mainly on God's veracity, for an external material world.

II

The origins of the other-minds problem are obscure, and a great service would be rendered by anyone who tracked them down. Among seventeenth- and early eighteenth-century philosophers Berkeley explicitly argues by analogy for the existence of other human minds,[5] and Locke "presume[s] it will be easily granted me, that there are such *ideas* in men's minds: every one is conscious of them in himself; and men's words and actions will satisfy him that they are in others."[6] This is not to say, however, that either one of these philosophers looks upon proving the existence of other minds as a major piece of philosophical business, though this disclaimer applies more to Locke than to Berkeley.

Descartes' numerous and varied remarks on the subject follow the same general pattern as those just mentioned. In a few instances the parallel with Locke's "presumption" is notable, but I cannot say that Locke's brief observation was made under the influence of Descartes. Whatever the relationship between Descartes and his British successors, it should not be surprising that their thinking about other minds follows similar channels. For while Berkeley rejects mind-matter dualism, his collections of (passive) ideas often play the role customarily assigned by earlier dualists to inert matter. And, more importantly, Descartes, Locke, and Berkeley share the so-called egocentric outlook, the view that the quest for knowledge begins with oneself and one's own experiential data. Given this outlook, each person faces the problem of extending this (essentially private) knowledge

[5] E.g., *Principles of Human Knowledge*, sections 140, 145, 148; *Dialogues Between Hylas and Philonous*, III [in *Berkeley's Philosophical Writings*, ed. D. M. Armstrong (New York), 1965), pp. 193–196]. Cf. *Principles*, Sect. 81 for a reference to non-human spirits whose faculties far exceed human minds.

[6] *Essay Concerning Human Understanding:* "Introduction," Sect. 8. Cf. Bk. IV, chap. 3, Sect. 27; Bk. IV, chap. 11, Sects. 9 & 12; and Bk. IV, chap. 21, Sect. 4. Cf. Berkeley's criticism of Locke's theory of language and general abstract ideas, *Principles of Human Knowledge, op. cit.,* "Introduction," Sect. 11.

to include, among other "things," minds like his own. An argument by analogy frequently has seemed to be a natural vehicle for this purpose.

These few historical references should help dispel the suspicion that it is anachronistic to construct an argument for other minds on behalf of a philosopher writing in the first half of the seventeenth century. The brunt of the case for construction must be borne, of course, by the passages I cite, with little or no criticism, from Descartes, and the hopefully non-Procrustean scheme I shall impose upon them.

Descartes' remarks, in his own Synopsis of the *Meditations*, about establishing the immortality of the soul might serve as a prologue to an argument for other minds. Included in the *Meditations*, he says, is "nothing . . . of which I do not possess very exact demonstrations," but what he does include will constitute the necessary groundwork for further demonstrations: ". . . I am obliged to follow a similar order to that made use of by geometers, which is to begin by putting forward as premises all those things upon which the proposition that we seek depends, before coming to any conclusion regarding it."[7] Nothing is said outright in the Synopsis about giving reasons for knowing that there are other minds, but that groundwork is provided for in the *Meditations* and elsewhere.[8]

III

Are there other human minds? Before laying out the argument it is important to see that this question, or something approaching it, is entertained by Descartes. A hint occurs in the *Discourse* (Section IV), after the *cogito* is produced, slipped in between the causal and the ontological arguments for God's existence: ". . . if there were any bodies in the world, or again any intelligences or other natures that were not entirely perfect, then their being must depend on his [i.e., God's] power, so that without him they could not subsist for a single moment."[9]

Doubt about other minds is more explicit in "The Search After

[7] HR, Vol. I, p. 140.

[8] The chief source for the construction is the *Meditations*, along with Descartes' "Replies" to the "Objections." The later *Principles of Philosophy* and *The Passions of the Soul*, together with the undated dialogue, "The Search After Truth," play a role in the argument that is largely ancillary. The earlier *Rules for the Direction of the Mind* and *Discourse on Method*, however, supply important material at crucial points.

[9] AG, p. 34.

Truth." One of the characters, Polyander, is persuaded to adopt methodical doubt as the best means of achieving knowledge. Quickly acquiring the Cartesian spirit he tells his companions that he is prepared to doubt that he is awake and that his senses are trustworthy. His conversion to the Cartesian method is summed up in these words: "In this way I shall be uncertain not only as to whether you are in the world, if a world exists, if there be a sun, but also whether I have eyes, ears, a body, even whether I talk with you, whether you address me, in short I shall doubt all things."[10]

Admittedly, a contemporary skeptic could do better than this. The expression of Cartesian doubt I have quoted may be little more than a variation on the question "Am I awake or dreaming?," covering everything including the existence of other minds. Other minds are not singled out for special skeptical treatment in the sense in which one might wonder (philosophically) if one's spouse or friend is a robot or really a person like oneself. Descartes addresses himself to a possibility approaching these distressing fantasies—see (4a) and (6) below—but never gives this skeptical doubt the sort of run for its money that it gets regarding bodies. Descartes' failure or reluctance to bring the question about other minds into sharper focus than he does finds its counterpart, inevitably, in the partial obscurity of the conclusion to his (constructed) argument.

The problem of other minds is suggested or provoked by at least one other claim made by Descartes, the claim that the proposition, "*One who is experiencing* (*cogitat*) cannot but exist while he is experiencing," is one of a number of "common notions," "axioms," or "eternal truths"; or, similarly, that the "principle," "Whatever experiences is or exists," "is learnt through his observing in his own case the impossibility of having experience without existing."[11] Unlike the *cogito* the first of these propositions, e.g., by itself does not assert (or "show") that anyone exists, but coupled with another, viz., "He/that man is experiencing (something or other)," it would entail that he/that man cannot but exist while he is experiencing. But how is one to discover that there are experiences occurring other than one's own, and that such experiences belong to some other mind?

The discovery will be made either directly, say by sensory or extrasensory perception, or indirectly by means of an inference. The first alternative, interestingly enough, does not seem to be taken as a logical impossibility by Descartes. He gives no reason, however, to believe that the direct perception of another mind is an empirical

[10] HR, Vol. I, p. 315. Cf. *Meditations*, II (AG, p. 67).
[11] *Principles*, Bk. I, Sect. xlix (AG, p. 191); AG, p. 299.

possibility in the world as it is. I excerpt the following passage regarding this alternative from his letter to Henry More, 15 April 1649:

> Being perceptible by the senses seems to be merely an external descrip-
> tion of sensible substance. Moreover it is not coextensive with such
> substance; if it concerns our senses, then it does not apply to the smallest
> particles of matter; if it concerns other senses such as we might imagine
> God to construct, it might well apply also to angels and souls. I find it no
> easier to imagine sensory nerves so fine that they could be moved by the
> smallest parts of matter than to imagine a faculty enabling our minds to
> sense or perceive other minds directly.[12]

It seems, then, that if one is to know about other minds one must infer
their existence, and, judging from the sample deductive argument
just given, the inference (if forthcoming at all) will be *non*-deductive.
For in order for the deduction to be sound, one will have to know
the premiss, "He/that man is experiencing (something or other),"
but if that premiss is known, then no *argument* will be needed to
prove that another mind exists.

Thus the problem is set for determining the sort of non-deductive
argument Descartes could rely on to justify belief in other minds.
Now for the constructed solution.

(1) *I exist: I know my own mind and my own thoughts, the ideas
(concepts) "self" and "consciousness" (cogitatio) being innate.* Descartes closes the Second Meditation by declaring: "I thus clearly
recognize that nothing is more easily or manifestly perceptible
to me than my own mind."[13] To know that he exists, that he is a
thinking, conscious thing, that he is having thoughts (experiences) of
one sort or another requires at least that he possess certain concepts
such as "self"[14] and "consciousness."[15] These Descartes accounts for
as seeming to come "from his own nature," i.e., they are innate.

An interesting difference may be noted here. Whereas in a letter,
dated August 1641, answering some objections to the *Meditations* put
forth by an unknown correspondent, he lists "the ideas of God, the

---

[12] *Descartes: Philosophical Letters*, tr. and ed. by Anthony Kenny (Oxford,
1970), p. 248. The reason for allowing for the direct perception of another mind is,
I take it, that ". . . in general we may affirm that God can do everything we can
comprehend, but not that He cannot do what we cannot comprehend; for it
would be rash to think our imagination reaches as far as His power does."
Letter to Mersenne, 15 April 1630 (AG, pp. 259–260).

[13] AG, p. 75. And from Rule III: ". . . anybody can see by mental intuition that
he himself exists, that he thinks . . ." (AG, p. 155).

[14] *Meditations*, III (AG, p. 83). See also the letter of August, 1641, AG, pp.
266–267, and letter to Mersenne (June 14, 1641), quoted in *Descartes: Philosophical Writings*, selected and tr. by Norman Kemp Smith (New York, 1958),
p. 197n.

[15] *Meditations*, III (AG, p. 79).

self, and all 'self-evident' truths" as examples of ideas in a mind "newly united to an infant body," he twice uses the phrase "my idea of myself" in Meditation III when showing how an idea such as 'angel" can be formed from the seemingly innate ideas of God and oneself. The all-important inclusion of the idea of *my*self, and not merely of *the* self, in the natural repository of the mind is accompanied by a teasing aside: "(as to which there can be no problem just now)."[16] Descartes apparently is mindful of the fact that he is about to launch into his first demonstration of God's existence and cannot as yet claim that the idea of himself does indeed come from God. But he may also dimly realize that, regardless of its origin, he can hardly proceed without this vital piece of conceptual equipment, that at this stage of the game he needs not only an underivable first proposition, the *cogito*, but some underivable concepts to match. The crucial one, of course, is not simply that of self, i.e., *any* self, but of *one's own* self.

All the same it may be wondered just what the idea of a mind, or self, in the Cartesian sense, is like. Gassendi objects that "Insofar as the ideas of things reputed to be immaterial are concerned, such as the idea of God, of an Angel, or of the human soul or mind, it is certain also that the ideas we do possess about these things are either corporeal or after the fashion of the corporeal, and drawn from the human form and, at other times, from the most subtle, the simplest and most imperceptible objects such as air or ether. . . ."[17] Descartes replies that the mind is "not imageable," that "in the true idea of mind, nothing is contained but thought and its attributes, of which none is corporeal."[18] What Descartes seems to be suggesting is that one knows what a mind is (what "mind" means), what thought is (what "thought" means), in the sense of knowledge by acquaintance—in this case issuing from a private ostensive definition. No description by itself will suffice, but then no conscious being has to rely solely on a description in order to have these ideas, or concepts.

(2) *There is a body that is* my *body*. Before concluding his proof for the existence of material things Descartes observes that there is 'some reason for holding that the body I called 'my body' by a special title really did belong to me more than any other body did. I could never really separate myself entirely from it, as I could from other bodies."[19] Descartes is led to say this from a consideration of bodily

[16] AG, p. 83.
[17] HR, Vol. II, p. 192.
[18] *Ibid.*, p. 230.
[19] *Meditations*, VI (AG, p. 112).

appetites and emotions, pains and titillations of pleasure. He feels or experiences these "in the body and on its account." After the general proof for bodies is concluded he is willing to proclaim that "there is no more explicit lesson of nature than that I have a body,"[20] and again, in support of this, he refers to sensations and the like that result from the body, *his* body, acting upon *his* mind.

(3) *There exist other bodies which by a "certain configuration of members and of other similar accidents" are human bodies.* At the end of the Synopsis Descartes offers his own assessment of the reasons given in Meditation VI from which the existence of material things is deduced:[21]

> Not that I judge them to be very useful in establishing that which they prove, to wit, that there is in truth a world, *that men possess bodies . . .* but because in considering these closely we come to see that they are neither so strong nor so evident as those arguments which lead us to the knowledge of our mind and of God. . . . [Italics added.]

It should be clear from the wording of this premiss that the words "human body" are no more than a convenient way of referring to a certain material shape resembling Descartes' own body. They must not be construed as begging the question in favor of such bodies being in fact conjoined to minds (possessed by men), thus making them bodies *of humans*.

(4a) *There could exist a functioning human body, i.e., a body like the body that I, a human being, have, but without a mind.* The human body may be considered "as a machine"—cf. the phrase "the human machine" occurring in "The Search After Truth"[22]—such that "even if there were no mind in it, it would still carry out all the operations that, as things are, do not depend on the command of the will, nor therefore, on the mind."[23]

In Discourse V this possibility is developed by imagining that God could create a human body, like ours externally and internally, "without placing in it, to begin with, any rational soul, or anything to serve as a vegetative or sensitive soul. . . ."[24]

---

[20] *Meditations*, VI (AG, p. 117). Cf. *Principles*, Bk. II, Sect. ii. Another, lesser reason perhaps is indicated in the Synopsis: "the human body, inasmuch as it differs from other bodies, is composed only of a certain configuration of members and of other similar accidents . . ." (HR, Vol. I, p. 141). Having reinstated to some degree the senses as sources of knowledge he can have veridical experiences of a body which by "figure or form" may be classified as a human body. An appeal to interaction with his mind might then establish this human body as *my* (i.e., Descartes') body.

[21] HR, Vol. I, pp. 142–143.

[22] *Ibid.*, p. 321.

[23] *Meditations*, VI (AG, p. 120).

[24] AG, p. 41. Cf. *Meditations*, VI (AG, p. 114).

(4b) *The relationship between the human body and the human mind is contingent.* This is the crucial presupposition behind (4a) and deserves separate treatment. To begin with there is the argument, in Meditation VI, that body and mind are "distinct." Replying to Arnauld's objection that this argument "proves too much," viz., that man's body is "merely the vehicle of spirit; whence follows the definition of man as a spirit that makes use of a body,"[25] Descartes asserts, not altogether convincingly, that he thought he "took sufficient care to prevent anyone thence inferring that *man was merely a spirit that makes use of a body . . .*" [italics in original].[26] The mind, he says, is "substantially united" with the body. Undoubtedly he is referring here to the famous passage in which he claims not to be present in his body merely as a pilot is present in a ship. "I am," he informs us, "most tightly bound to it, and as it were mixed up with it, so that I and it form a unit."[27] Nevertheless mind and body are assuredly distinct because God can separate one from the other.[28]

There is something unsatisfactory about basing body-mind contingency on God's abilities, for this is the sort of "explanation" that explains nothing at all—particularly in Descartes' case given his incredible contention that God has created the so-called eternal truths, that they are subject to divine power and not the other way round. We do slightly better by looking at the *Principles*[29] where it is affirmed that "we are certain that he [God] can do whatever we distinctly understand." Descartes goes on to say that each of us, as a conscious being, "can in thought exclude from himself any other substance, whether conscious or extended." And finally, whatever things God has "conjoined" or "compounded" as a unity remain separable by God and so are really distinct.

Fortunately we can do better still by bringing to bear on (4a and b) the discussion of simple and compound "natures" in Rule XII.[30] The conjunction of simple natures with one another is "either necessary or contingent"—this key phrase occurring in all major English translations: AG, HR, and Kemp Smith. Some examples of necessary conjunction are: figure and extension, motion and duration, four-

---

[25] HR, Vol. II, p. 84.

[26] *Ibid.*, p. 102.

[27] *Meditations*, VI (AG, p. 117). Cf. Letter to Princess Elizabeth, June 28, 1643 (AG, p. 281).

[28] Cf. *Meditations*, VI (AG, p. 114).

[29] Bk. I, Sect. lx (AG, pp. 193–194).

[30] *Rules* (AG, pp. 171–178, esp. p. 174). This topic is the source of many vexing problems that are tangential to the subject of this paper. See, e.g., Leonard G. Miller, "Descartes, Mathematics, and God," *The Philosophical Review*, vol. 66 (1957), pp. 451–465.

plus-three and seven; also, "from Socrates' assertion that he doubts
everything there is a necessary consequence 'therefore he understands
at least what he doubts'." One of each of the foregoing pairs is "implicitly contained in the concept of the other"; "we cannot distinctly
conceive of either if we judge that they are separated." Not so, however, with contingent combinations "as when we say that a body is
animated, that a man is clothed, etc."[31]

(5) *I can (and do) have ideas of other men, though there may exist
no other men like myself.* The source of this premiss is the same as for
a portion of (1). The two relevant short paragraphs from Meditation
III may be quoted in full:[32]

> Now my ideas include, besides my idea of myself (as to which there can
> be no problem just now), various ideas representing God, inanimate
> corporeal objects, angels, animals, and finally other men like myself. As
> regards ideas standing for other men, or animals, or angels, I can easily
> see that they could be formed from my ideas of myself, corporeal
> objects, and God; even if there were in the world no men but me, no
> animals, and no angels.

Note that unlike the idea of the human mind, which is not imageable
—see reply to Gassendi in (1)—the idea of a man, or human being, is
a mental picture of an object.[33] So it is not only the hard and fast
distinction between the human body and the human mind that
permits Descartes to entertain the disquieting possibility that there
might exist human bodies without minds. It is also the possibility of
having in one's own mind ideas of other men, i.e., ideas of intimate
mixtures of mind and body—see reply to Arnauld in (4b)—without
there being any other men. It is difficult for Descartes to prevent the
conflation of the ideas of (human) mind and of man, but it is important to realize that this distinction is precisely what he insists upon.

(6) *But, in actuality, there exist "real men," intimate conjunctions
of human bodies and human minds, who are distinguishable from robots
and from brutes.* A machine "with the organs and appearances of a
monkey" could not be distinguished in nature from a monkey, but
machines "resembling our bodies, and imitating our actions as far
as is morally possible" *could* be distinguished from "real men" in
two ways: (i) a robot "could never use words or other constructed
signs, as we do to declare our thoughts to others." A machine could

---

[31] Cf. *Meditations*, II, where it is allowed that the hats and coats "seen" to cover
men are, strictly speaking, *judged* to cover them. This judgment may be mistaken,
for it is possible that the garments cover automata.

[32] AG, p. 83.

[33] *Meditations*, III (AG, p. 78).

be made to utter words, e.g., "if it is touched in one part, it asks what you want to say to it, and if touched in another, it cries out that it is hurt; but not that it should be made as to arrange words variously in response to the meaning of what is said in its presence, as even the dullest men can do."[34] (We are not told why touch but not sound is causally efficacious regarding the verbal responses of robots.) (ii) It is allowed that robots could do some things as well as or better than we do, but "they would infallibly fail in others, revealing that they acted not from knowledge but only from the disposition of their organs."[35] Reason serves in all kinds of circumstances, but these organs need a special arrangement for each special action. It is "morally impossible" that a machine could contain enough arrangements for it to match the variety of human actions.

It is instructive to see how Descartes recognizes the differences between men and brutes. Again, he uses the criteria of language and behavior, the former being of greater significance, so it seems. A few birds can be taught to utter words, but unlike us they do so without "any sign of being aware of what they say."[36] Even handicapped men such as deaf mutes invent a sign language for themselves, but brutes have not invented any language and so are "wholly lacking" in reason. The similarity of animals' organs and ours is noted by Descartes. Thus the absence of an animal language could be accounted for only on the supposition that brutes lack the requisite mental backing for language. Hence it may be inferred that the use of language, in varied circumstances, is quite sufficient for Descartes to ascribe thinking to a being.

An interesting objection to Descartes' view of animals is posed in the sixth set of the Objections. Descartes denies that a dog, say, knows that it is running or thinking, but perhaps a dog would judge the same of us: "For . . . you [Descartes] do not behold the dog's internal mode of operation, just as he is not directly aware of yours. . . ."[37] The reply[38] is that those who ascribe thought to animals talk as if "they could take up their station in the animals' hearts," whereas he (Descartes) has a *proof* that brutes possess no thought. But more important is the reply to the supposition that man is without sensation and understanding, that all his actions can be explained by means of "dynamical mechanisms" as is the case with animals:[39]

[34] Discourse V (AG, pp. 41–42).
[35] *Ibid.*
[36] *Ibid.*
[37] HR, Vol. II, p. 235.
[38] *Ibid.*, pp. 244–245.
[39] *Ibid.*

For surely we cannot help at every moment experiencing within us that we think; nor can anyone infer from the fact that it has been shown that the animate brutes can discharge all these operations entirely without thought, that he therefore does not think. . . . Far more will be found who, if it is conceded *that thought is not to be distinguished from bodily motion,* will with much better reason conclude that it is the same thing in us and in them, since they notice in them all corporeal movements as in us. . . . [Italics in original.]

But, as he points out in Discourse V, the use of language and certain sorts of behavior do serve to distinguish us from brutes. Brutes being automata (and Descartes admitting that there may be no way of telling the two apart), the same reasoning serves to distinguish us from robots. Now we need only fill in the obvious: if there are criteria which *not being met* permit me to distinguish myself, a thinking, speaking agent, from brutes and robots, then those same criteria *when met* must permit me, given the foregoing premisses of the constructed argument, to infer the existence of other thinking, speaking agents like myself. (This assumes that the criteria in question represent both necessary and sufficient conditions for distinguishing men from non-men. Descartes, I believe, meant them to play this dual role.)

IV

Some words now about the sort of inference with which Descartes concludes that there exist other human minds conjoined with human bodies. The final move in this construction is not so clearly defined as one could wish for. As a starter there is a veracious deity who is the *sine qua non* for all "perfect knowledge.": "And now it becomes possible for countless things to be clearly known and certain to me; both about God himself and other intellectual beings, and about the whole field of corporeal nature that is the subject-matter of pure mathematics."[40] How, specifically, does one clearly and certainly know about "other intellectual beings"? Not, I have maintained, by an argument sufficiently analogous to that proving the existence of material things. It is not simply an argument from effect to cause. Copleston is undoubtedly right to assign God a role in the unstated argument for other minds, for Descartes says that without knowledge of God he cannot be certain of anything. The last paragraph of Meditation V, just quoted, settles that. There are, however, snags in

[40] *Meditations,* V (AG, p. 108).

pressing the analogy with the argument for bodies too closely. In Meditation VI Descartes starts with his clear and distinct ideas of material things (extension, flexibility, and the like), and then by a series of side arguments eliminates himself, God, and (presumably) the evil genius from contention as the cause of those ideas. That leaves material things themselves. Descartes' qualification in the Synopsis aside,[41] the complete argument for the existence of bodies is meant as a deduction or quasi-deduction. That is, he seems there to be making the Orwellian pronouncement that all deductions are strong and evident, but some, like those for God's existence, are stronger and more evident than others, such as the one for bodies.

An argument for other minds, by contrast, does not begin simply with clear and distinct ideas of other minds. Remember, they are not images. Of course one has ideas of self and of thought, but the factor of ownership intrudes. What I start with are ideas of *my* self and of *my* thoughts. What would it be like to have an idea of *another* self, of *his* thought? Well, one has ideas of bodies, other human bodies, and *another* body is one that at least does not have the intimate causal relationship to one's own mind that one's own body has. Then, by a series of steps, one gets to the stage where a mind is ascribed to another such body by virtue of an analogy with one's own mind and body. But this comes about, I have argued, not merely by eliminating God, etc., from the list of possible causes for the idea of another mind.

Furthermore, on Copleston's interpretation, ruling out oneself as the source of ideas of other minds is a rather precarious operation. With respect to ideas of bodies, Descartes argues that sensation is inessential to himself (as a thinking, unextended thing), and thus, while apparently involved in receiving such ideas, he cannot be the cause of those ideas. But his own self, a thinking thing, cannot likewise be eliminated as the cause of ideas of "other minds." It is just the sort of thing that *is* adequate for the idea of a mind. (In the Scholastic jargon that Descartes uses, the existence of the Cartesian self has the right degree of formal reality for the objective reality of the idea of another self.)

No, it seems that Descartes' argument for other minds would take the form, not of a straight causal argument to determine the source of ideas of other minds, but rather, once the having of ideas of *men*, other men, other human beings, is accounted for, of justifying the belief that there are such men. This will require giving reasons for

[41] See Synopsis of *Meditations*, HR, Vol. I, pp. 142–143; and cf. above, n. 20.

ascribing (or conjoining) minds to bodies, for asserting that there are human bodies animated by human minds. That is to say, Descartes begins his philosophical enterprise with the *cogito* and with some incorrigible data, his own ideas. He tries to move *directly* from some of these ideas (and the knowledge that God exists) to the existence of bodies by means of a causal argument. But given his notion of a special but nevertheless contingent relation between body and mind—the two are "substantially united" he says—the idea of the body intervenes. Minds are then conjoined with these bodies by means of an argument somewhat like that from analogy.

It is apparent that I have a reservation about assigning a full-blown argument from analogy to Descartes, for such an argument would seem to fall short of his requirements for knowledge, met only by intuition and deduction. He himself regards the reasons he gives for distinguishing "real men" from machines—see (6) above—as establishing the *moral* impossibility that machines could duplicate human actions. Supposedly, then, it is not *metaphysically* impossible that a machine could behave as men behave. This means that Descartes' belief in the existence of other men does not rest solely on intuition and deduction, for both intuition and sound deductive arguments are sufficiently powerful to banish metaphysical doubts.[42] It would be rash to conclude from this, however, that Descartes' argument for other minds is clearly and obviously analogical in form. It may simply not fit into those neat types of inference that so transfix formal logicians.[43]

Adding to my perplexity is the fact that he is willing to employ "conjecture" with respect to the compounding of judgments. Views that are compounded in this way "are not misleading, so long as we regard them only as probable and never assert them as truth; they actually add to our stock of information."[44] A good example of Descartes' use of conjecture, where he actually argues by analogy, is

[42] Cf. A. Kenny, *Descartes, A Study of His Philosophy* (New York, 1968), p. 182.

[43] For example, how is one to unpack this remark, made in a letter to Princess Elizabeth (28 June, 1643), concerning the primitive notion of the union between soul and body? ". . . it is just by means of ordinary life and conversation, by abstaining from meditating and from studying things that exercise the imagination, that one learns to conceive the union of soul and body" (AG, p. 280). Insofar as this pertains to *conceiving* of such a union it is relevant to step (5) in my argument. Insofar as the union is *learned* from ordinary life and conversation it suggests an inference. But if the latter, can it be a straightforwardly analogical inference when the soul-body union is primitive? I am not altogether grateful to Prof. Van de Pitte for drawing my attention to this passage.

[44] See *Rules*, XII regarding compound judgments stemming from impulse, conjecture, and deduction (AG, p. 176).

to be found in the *Principles*.[45] A conclusion is reached about the insensible parts of natural bodies by arguing from an analogy with the sensible parts of bodies, especially machines.

A case closer to the topic of this paper, illustrating the probabilistic aspect of conjectures, comes from *Passions of the Soul:* "How one and the same cause may excite different passions in different men."[46] Ignoring the obsolete physiology, Descartes' point is that "the same impression which a terrifying object makes on the gland, and which causes fear in certain men, may excite in others courage and confidence." Passions such as fear, courage, and confidence are contingently related to objects and to behavior (and supposedly to "gland states"); consequently one should want to discover how it is that he can know that another person is fearful when he, himself, is courageous and confident. Surely not by examining a person's pineal gland or brain. According to Discourse V—see above under (6)—it would be by observing gross actions and by language.

But how do I know that the ideas or thoughts lying hidden behind your words are like the ideas that I perceive to lie behind my own similar utterances? One's answer to this question is decisive and broaches the matter of private objects and private languages. The argument by analogy, or whatever we choose to call it, is implicitly used by Descartes to get round the privacy of objects, but if this seems at all plausible within the context of his system it is because he assumes uncritically that the language we use in probing the private minds and thoughts of others is public, public in the sense that it can be, and is, used for communication between different minds. And if it is a vehicle for communication, then language is teachable and learnable. It is surely debatable, however, whether privacy of the first sort, in which the meanings of words are the private objects to which they refer, does not imply, *contra* Descartes, privacy of the second sort, a language that is understandable only to its user. And more so, that if a language of the second sort is impossible, then so is a Cartesian language of the first sort. If all this be granted, then the reasoning Descartes uses to tell men from machines is a non-starter. If it is not granted, if a Cartesian private-object language is a viable means of communication as Descartes implicitly thinks, then we have at least one good reason for understanding why Descartes and

---

[45] *Principles*, Bk. IV, Sect. cciii (AG, pp. 236–237). Comment on Rule I begins: "Whenever men notice some similiarity between two things, they are wont to ascribe to each, even in those respects in which the two differ, what they have found to be true of the other" (HR, Vol. I, p. 1). But there is no hint in what Descartes says that this tendency to ascribe may be relevant to the problem of other minds.

[46] First Part, xxxix (HR, Vol. I, p. 349).

his successors do not regard the other-minds problem as the big problem it has become for us. A multitude of private egos in their epistemological predicaments are really not in desperate straits if it is supposed that they share a common language and a common schema. The resolution of this matter, however, is another story going far beyond the task I set myself in this paper.[47] In any event, Descartes' argument for other minds, as I construe it, does serve to bring this post-Wittgensteinian problem into focus within a traditional setting.[48]

San Fernando Valley State College

[47] See John Turk Saunders and Donald F. Henze, *The Private-Language Problem* (New York, 1967), chap. 1.

[48] This paper was discussed at the Philosophy Department Colloquium of San Fernando Valley State College and read to the Philosophy Department, University of Alberta at Edmonton. I am grateful to members of both departments for their helpful and challenging comments.

Meaning and Feeling
MORELAND PERKINS*

SENSUALIST: I believe that the meaning of every word we use to refer to one of our shared sensuous feelings is in part constituted by the shared feeling, itself, somewhat as this same meaning is in part constituted by the shared practice which is the use of the word.

BEHAVIORIST: How are you using the phrase, "sensuous feeling"?

SENSUALIST: Somewhat oddly: to refer to those sensory experiences we call feelings, but also to refer to sensory experiences generally; for example, to pain, a sensory experience we call a feeling, but also to the visual impression of scarlet, a sensory experience we do not call a feeling. So what I said about shared sensuous feeling I meant to say about all of our shared sensory experiences. For economy's sake I want a single word, and I think the word "feeling" is less misleading, as to denotation, than the word "experience" would be.

BEHAVIORIST: Why not use the word "sensation"?

SENSUALIST: With respect to denotation, and as traditionally used by philosophers, that would perhaps be the best choice. So you may imagine "sensation" replacing "feeling," if you wish. I prefer the word "feeling" because its grammar—the company it keeps—better suits my present purposes. Choice of words aside, I take it you disagree with my thesis?

BEHAVIORIST: Of course.

SENSUALIST: What is your argument?

BEHAVIORIST: Only our behavior can provide a mechanism of reference for the words of our language. Referring to things with words can be accomplished only through behaving. The reason is that only what comes into public view can play a role in communication of sense, and therefore in communication of reference. And the obvious behavior to choose for this role as mechanism of reference is the *use* of words by the speakers of the language to which the words belong.

* This essay was first conceived and composed while its author held a fellowship in the Humanities Center at The Johns Hopkins University. It was reconceived and recomposed while he held a Faculty Research Award from the General Research Board of the Graduate School of The University of Maryland. The appearance in this dialogue of alleged views or words of actual persons constitutes the author's adaptation to his purposes of the general purport only (as he all too fallibly remembers it) of views expressed or words uttered by these persons.

But it is only through the meanings words have that combinations of words succeed in referring to things: the meanings of words are the mechanism of reference for words. It follows that the meanings words have are constituted by the patterns of behavior which comprise the use of these words. Meaning is use, which is behavior.

Feeling, however, does not itself come into public view. Sensory experience does not come into public view. And neither does the memory of either one of these. So humankind's shared feelings, and memory of feelings, cannot play a role in the communication of meaning and reference. Meaning and reference of the kind that can be communicated by language cannot be accomplished even in part by shared feelings and other sensory experiences.

SENSUALIST: But what is your reason for saying that only what comes into public view can play a role in communication of meaning and reference? What role is in question? If the role is that of vehicle of communication, I am disposed to say that of course the principle is true: that a vehicle of public communication has got to be open to public view. But the role here in question is not that of vehicle but of communicated sense, or meaning. How do you prove that this role can be played only by something open to the view of the public?

BEHAVIORIST: You make my task appear too difficult, by misstating it. Communicated sense is the upshot of communication; it is not a role played in communication.

SENSUALIST: I grant it. I retract. For the moment, anyhow. But now how is one to state your theory? You say that the vehicle must be public. This tells us nothing about what it is that makes the vehicle communicate a sense. Its mere publicity alone will not do the job. What does?

BEHAVIORIST: If you discover the whole nature of the public vehicle, you have discovered the mechanism of reference; there is no more to unearth. And the whole vehicle of communication is the words, phrases, and sentences, together with their use, both of which are open to public view. All that there is to meaning and to reference is to be found there.

SENSUALIST: It may be so. But what is the argument? *I* say that, in addition to the words and their use, our common, shared sensuous experiences play a part in constituting the communicated sense of some words—in making some of our words mean what they mean; therefore our sensory experiences help effect these words' reference. Indeed, if we are going to speak of the "whole vehicle" of communication, then we should speak of feeling as part of this vehicle: my feeling is sometimes a kind of vehicle of your words' meaning getting communicated to me, and vice-versa; you and I both recognize this fact when we say, "You will not understand what I am saying unless you have felt what I am referring to."

BEHAVIORIST: Speak for yourself. I . . .

SENSUALIST: I was trying to avoid prejudice. But let me finish. Suppose I say that the role of feeling is exactly like the role of use, except that one person's feeling is not open to another's view, whereas his use is. And I add that this qualification is no hindrance, since although we cannot observe them we all *know* a good deal about one another's sensuous experiences and feelings.

Indeed, there is a doubt about the complete publicity of the *use* of words. For we can use words to refer to what is not observable, for example to the spin of an electron. Can the use we make of words that makes words refer to something unobservable be itself wholly observable? In truth, I wonder if *any*thing does its work wholly in the open. Isn't there some folly in supposing that the complete working of any *mechanism* is wholly open to public inspection, having in mind, as you do, the non-scientific public?

BEHAVIORIST: Think of it this way. Meaning something by words and referring to something are accomplishments. They are things done; they involve actions. They require, necessarily, a development in time, something headed for, and something reached. There has to be a purpose, and a method of execution of the purpose. There has to be an end in view, and a technique for accomplishing the end. Exactly the same things can be said of using a word, or a phrase, or a sentence. So explaining how it is that words mean, or that we mean things with words, by saying that it is through our use of words, is appropriate. But feeling is not doing; it is no form of action. So we cannot, even in part, explain how we mean things with words by citing a role for our sensuous feelings.

SENSUALIST: That is a good answer to my suggestion that the role of feeling in constituting some words' meanings is like the role of use. Using words is a way of behaving. And the role of feeling in making some words mean what they mean cannot be the same as the role of behaving. But as an argument against saying that our shared sensuous feeling helps make some words mean what they mean, your reply is unsatisfactory. It proves that if we had to settle for only one, feeling or use, then we should have to choose use. It shows that feeling can in no instance be the whole story. But I should not want to suggest that it ever is. What your argument does not show is that shared feeling and other sensory experience cannot play an indispensable role in making some words mean what they mean. Not everything that plays a part in accomplishing an action need be another action. Wittgenstein's example of a language in which color samples play an indispensable role (as "instruments" of the language) might be useful here. *Their* role in making the words of his imagined language mean what they mean is different from the role of the *use* of these color samples and from the role of the use of the words of the language; and it is different as well from the roles of the mere words. It is the same, I say, for sensuous feeling, or for our shared sensory experiences; their role in making some words mean what they mean is not like the role of our *use* of the words, and it is not like the role of the *words* that are used.

BEHAVIORIST: The analogy you suggest would help with the objection you are meeting if the analogy were valid. But there is a difficulty. The color samples can be *used* by the speakers of the language; it is this that makes them "instruments" of the language. But sensory experiences and feelings are not something that can be *used*. So the role of feeling in making some words mean what they mean is unintelligible. This is my central objection. This is the heart of the trouble with feelings. If they are not a way of *doing* something, then it must be possible for something to *be done with* them, if they are to play a role in making words mean what they mean. But it is not possible to do anything with a feeling.

SENSUALIST: There are two elements in your objection, one well taken, the other, I think, mere dogma. You are absolutely right in saying that the role of feeling cannot be like the role of Wittgenstein's color samples. I meant—well, I *now* mean the comparison to help only as getting us away from the idea that actions alone can contribute to actions. A color sample is a mere thing; it *has* to be used if it is to come to something in a human affair. A feeling, a sensory experience, is quite another matter. In the same sense of the word "use," it cannot be used. It is *had*, by users of other things. So far, I agree with you.

BEHAVIORIST: Thank you.

SENSUALIST: Not at all. Thank *you*. But your further contention, that in order to play a role in making words mean what they mean, a candidate for a role must either qualify as a use of something or as something that is put to a use, enunciates as self-evident a principle that does not appear to me at all evident. Indeed, one could say that we *do* use feeling to understand words. After all, we do. But this is doubtless a use of "use" that should not be permitted when the meaning of words is being identified with the use of words. So I am inclined to say, simply, that if feeling is neither a use nor an instrument, then so much the worse for the principle that only uses and instruments play parts in making words mean what they mean.

BEHAVIORIST: You are not easy. But you are dead wrong in your stubbornness. So I shall make one more effort. Do not interrupt. I am going to give you my understanding of an argument I overheard in a conversation between a philosopher who shares my view of this matter, Bernard Gert, and someone with a blind spot exactly like yours. Perhaps it will help.

SENSUALIST: I am all ears. I know Gert.

BEHAVIORIST: The primary confusion of a philosopher like you, who believes that the shared sensory experience of the users of a language helps effect the reference of words that refer to this experience, by entering into the meanings of these words, is his at least implicit belief in the following confused proposition: that the referent of a word—what the word can correctly be used to refer to—determines the meaning the word has in the language. For it is evident, once it is conceded that a sensation is neither a use nor an instrument used, that the only way a sensation can "enter into the meaning" of a word that refers to it is in the role of *that which is referred to* by means of the correct use of the word. What you rather grandly call the sensuous feeling, pain, and I call simply the sensation, pain, could figure in the meaning of the word "pain" only as that to which speakers refer when they use the word "pain" correctly. But neither the referent of a "sensation word" nor of any other word can determine, let alone enter into, the meaning of the word. For if it could, then meaning could be given to a sensation-word merely by associating a certain sound or inscription with the sensation and attending, the while, to the sensation. But this cannot be done. We associate "ouch" with the sensation, pain, and our attention is generally focused upon this sensation while saying "ouch." Yet "ouch" does not thereby acquire meaning, in the required sense: by uttering it we do not refer to pain. Correctly used, "pain" refers to pain; "ouch" does not. The reason is that meaning of the kind that enables a word—in consort with other words—to refer arises only from the word's receiving a special kind of use in the language. Provide the right kind of use in the language for the word "pain" and you provide it with meaning of the sort that helps effect a reference. Whereas "staring at" the pain and uttering the sound "pān" carries you no way at all in the direction of giving this sound a meaning: for all we know you may "intend" to speak of pleasure, by a kind of "rule of opposition," in uttering the sound in conjunction with that sensation. Until you give the sound a use, assign it a role in the language, you have given it no meaning. Assign the role, and the meaning is not only determined, it is thereby constituted: the role of the word in the language *is* the word's meaning. Therefore the referents, the things that are referred to, play no part in the achievement of ours that consists in our meaning things by the words we use. Consequently nothing is to be learned about the meaning of a sensation word by "examining" or otherwise "inspecting" or attending to or being aware of the sensation itself. We mean by a given word a certain (kind of) sensation only in virtue of mastering a use for this word, a use by whose means we single out as belonging to a kind, and refer to, the instances of this sensation: this mastery of a use *constitutes* our meaning by this word a certain sensation. Neither the instances of the sensation referred to nor its properties play, themselves, *any* role in the achievement that consists in meaning by a word or phrase this very kind of sensation and in referring to examples of it. Therefore the fact that one has had the sensation to which a word like "pain" refers has nothing whatever to do with one's understanding the meaning of this word, or with how one means the word in using it; this is determined solely by one's mastery of the use of the word in the language to which it belongs.

SENSUALIST: I have listened, and I am comforted. The argument is a total failure.

BEHAVIORIST: You cannot be serious.

SENSUALIST: I do not joke about pain. But one point I concede—will you hear me out?

BEHAVIORIST: Go ahead.

SENSUALIST: I concede this: that if one says, as I do, that a shared sensuous feeling or experience enters into the meaning of the words used especially to refer to it, then one has by implication said that the referents of a "sensation word" help determine, even help constitute the meaning of this word.

And so they do! But to appreciate this rather neglected truth it will be best to begin with words that are commonly used to refer to ordinary material objects. Before doing this, however, let me call your attention to a peculiarity of your way of formulating *my* thesis. Regularly you spoke of a *single* person's feeling helping to determine or constitute what he means by a word. But I have spoken only of a (kind of) feeling *as* shared by the race of men who use the language; it is only of this widespread feeling that I have said that it enters into the meaning of the word used by a whole race of men to refer to the feeling. Now think: if instead of saying, as you did, ". . . the fact that one has had the sensation to which a given word . . . refers has nothing whatever to do with . . . how one means the word, in using it," you had said, as you should have done, "The fact that from time immemorial the race of men who speak the language to which a given word belongs have all commonly suffered or enjoyed the sensation to which this word refers has nothing whatever to do with how those who use this language mean the word in using it," would you not have been more skeptical of your own utterance?

BEHAVIORIST: It does seem a more stunning declaration.

SENSUALIST: Mind you, I do not mean to deny that the individual's feeling does play a role in constituting his meaning and in effecting his reference. After all, what a race of men accomplish requires single laborers, and only individuals suffer and enjoy.

But now let us examine a related question; let us consider the case for saying that the *referent* of a "material-object word" helps to determine and even, literally, enters into the meaning of the word.

Take the word "table." It has meaning. And it has, on certain occasions of its use, a referent—at least, when it is taken together with the words associated with it in the sentence in which it figures it can be said to refer to a particular table. Now in order to get some of the meanings commonly given to the word "meaning" separated from one another in our discussion, let us distinguish, from the kind of meaning that interests *you*, three other more traditional kinds—they make pretty blunt instruments, but we have not aimed at technical precision in this conversation, and I think they will roughly serve our generalizing purposes. For convenience, then, call the "extension" of the word "table" the set of its actual referents when it is correctly used: the set of tables. Call one of its "referents" any single object that is correctly called a table. Call the "signification" of the word "table" the properties a thing must have in order that it can correctly be called a table, but do not ask me to make up the complete list of properties. Now say that the word "table" has meaning exactly in so far as it has a use; and by that I mean this: what speakers of the English language *do* that *constitutes* their coming to mean something in uttering the word "table" (and hence makes the word "table" have meaning in English) is to give the word "table" a use in English. In coming to give a word a use we succeed in giving the word its meaning—we succeed in meaning something by using the word. Meaning, in *this* sense, *is* use. *Now* we can say that it is solely in virtue of the fact that the word "table" has been given a use in English, and is in *this* sense given meaning, that it has the signification that it has, and therefore that the fact that it has the extension it has is a consequence of its having been given this use: the use determines the signification which determines the extension (on single occasions, the referent).

Now the objection of yours that I have to answer, as applied to the word "table" (a material-thing word substituting for a sensation word), amounts to this contention: "Neither the set of all real tables, nor any subset of them, nor any single table, neither the extension nor any part of the extension, nor any single referent of the word 'table' enters into, helps constitute, or even helps determine the meaning, in the sense of the use, of the word 'table.' Moreover, what holds of the extension, and of each referent singly, holds as well of the signification of 'table': the actual properties of some objects which are signified by our calling these objects tables do not themselves either enter into or determine, in whole or in part, the meaning, in the sense of the use, of the word 'table.' On the contrary: it is the use in English of the word 'table' that determines what the signification, what the extension, and what the referent of each occasion of the word's correct application to a material object shall be. It follows that one gives no meaning to the sound 'tābl' by associating it with actual tables, that is, by merely uttering it consistently in the presence of a table and concentrating one's attention upon the table that is before one; also it follows that nothing can be learned about the meaning of the word 'table' by inspecting tables. What has to be examined or attended to in order to learn the meaning of the word 'table' is the use in English of the word 'table,' not the tables themselves."

Do I understand the argument?

BEHAVIORIST: You appear to.

SENSUALIST: Then listen. It is preposterous to say that I can learn nothing about the use of the word "table" by examining tables. (And it is equally so no matter how much or how little language I have already mastered.) A man with eyes to see with who refuses to examine with his eyes the things people refer to by means of the word "table" in order to help himself learn how the word "table" is used in English would be a fool. For people with eyes one phase or dimension of the process of learning the meaning of a word that has visually observable referents—in the sense of learning the word's use in the language—is the visual examination of those referents. And the relevance, for the same purpose, of the use of other sense-organs is equally evident. I do not say this is the only way one can learn the use of a word, any more than I say that a man without eyes cannot learn the use of the word "table." But surely it is characteristically a part of the process of learning the use of a word. So any analysis of meaning which entails that this cannot be true is surely false.

BEHAVIORIST: I confess that what you say about learning the use of a word does sound plausible. Some of the argument I gave may have to be given up. But I am not now so certain that that argument *was* entailed by the behavioristic theory of meaning, by the conception that meaning something and therefore referring to something by a word constitutes an achievement involving an action, with a purpose, and a technique, and all the rest of the theory that meaning is use. And I do not see that you have established that the referent of a word does enter into the word's meaning: that a material object referred to should *itself* constitute part of the very meaning, hence part of the use of the word—part of the very mechanism by which the word refers to that very object—*this* is a preposterous idea.

SENSUALIST: Not at all! In fact I am certain that if a disinterested third person were listening to this conversation he would by now see clearly how necessary it is to say that actual wooden and aluminum and steel and stone tables do themselves enter into the very meaning —that is, into the use in English, into the very semantic mechanism effecting the reference—of the word "table." And I, personally, am delighted with the realization that having started out intending to bring feelings into the very meanings of some words, I have ended up making, as well, some words' meanings consist of things like solid, wooden tables. Although no behaviorist, I am, as it happens, a materialist—but this is by the way.

A use in a "natural" language like English of a word having a set of material objects for its extension is—*you* insist on it—a pattern of behavior on the part of those who use the language. And what can this be but a pattern in which the utterance of the word is brought into a complex connection with the utterance of other words, and with still other complex patterns of behavior, *and* with actual instances of the kind of object to which the word is correctly applied?

You are the behaviorist. You stress the thesis that this use in English of the word "table" must be conceived to consist in overt action having a goal and a technique of realizing the goal—and surely you should be the last to deny that this action requires a supporting environment of relevant material objects. Would an account of a rat's pattern of purposive behavior in a maze be complete that left out of the pattern the maze itself! How would this account go, pray?

Similarly, the use in its language of a material-object word cannot be characterized without speaking of the *enabling* (hence causal) role —in this use—of the material objects themselves (the tables, for example), which *support* the behavior, and which function as the several referents of the word. The *whole* mechanism of reference whereby the word "table" refers to tables includes the part the tables themselves play in this transaction. Of course—

MR. BART GRUZALSKI: Pardon me, sir—won't this whole mechanism of reference, by your account, turn out to include human breathing as well?

SENSUALIST: Hmmm. . . .

PROFESSOR LARS SVENONIUS: The presence of the breathing, and the mode of its presence, is common to all instances of using words, as well as to all other forms of behavior, whereas the presence of the tables—or, at the least, the mode of their presence—within the practice of using the word "table" is perhaps not repeated within any other word's "defining practice."

SENSUALIST: The question was good, the answer still better, and I thank you both. And I add: the table's role in the practice of using the word "table" also differs from the role breathing has within the same practice in virtue of its being that *part* of the enabling mechanism of this practice which *is* the referent of the word whose meaning is established through this practice.

I continue. Of course, as I started to remark, one can say that the tables' role in the use in English of the word "table" is a rather passive one. And so is the role of bottles, in the practice of labeling bottles, rather a passive one. But—despite the differences there are between the use of a word to refer to a table and the labeling of bottles—you might as well say that actual bottles do not enter into the practice of labeling bottles as say that actual tables do not enter into the use in English of the word "table." I conclude that real tables enter into the meaning of the word "table."

You see where I have come. I now suggest that there is no good reason why the substance of what I have just demonstrated does not hold equally true of the kind of word or phrase that is used to refer to a pain or to a visual impression of a scarlet expanse, except that instead of speaking of examining or observing the referent we shall need, generally, to speak of having it or of feeling it and perhaps at most of giving our attention to it, in the first-person case, and otherwise of observing *that* it is there. Switching my analogy: you might as well say that the pains of hospital patients do not play a part in the practice of nursing as say that the pains of speakers and auditors do not enter into the use in English of the word "pain." I conclude. . . .

BEHAVIORIST: But *I* should say *both* of those things! The unobservability, the public inaccessibility, the privacy of pains and the like prevents them from occupying the place in the use and hence in the meaning of words which you have, perhaps, demonstrated belongs to tables and to *their* like.

SENSUALIST: I am—I admit it—a little impatient with the privacy of sensations. Not that I deny *some* form of it. Far from it: in its place it needs emphasis. And on another occasion I will argue the fine points with you. But listen. Be simple.

Of what earthly phenomenon do we take more systematic account than of the pains of other human beings—and of ourselves? To what phenomenon is human behavior more vividly and sensitively attuned than to the occurrence of acute pain in another human being? Perhaps "sensual pleasure" would be an answer!

Think of chemists and neurologists and pharmacologists, of surgeons and anaesthetists and nurses, of friends and parents and lovers. Surely it is silly to pretend that our own and others' pains do not themselves enter as commonly into the mechanism of our shared behavioral practice of coping with them, generally, and, more particularly, into the mechanism of the shared practice of referring to them, as tables and chairs enter into our practice of coping with, and, more particularly, referring to *them*. Isn't this silly?

BEHAVIORIST: It does sound rather. Yet I am not convinced.

SENSUALIST: Cannot sensual pleasure, itself, cause a man to smile, to sigh and to take action aimed at preserving the pleasure?

BEHAVIORIST: Yes.

SENSUALIST: Then sensual pleasure, itself, can constitute at least part of the cause of a man's reporting that he feels the pleasure?

BEHAVIORIST: Yes.

SENSUALIST: And since I may respond to another's report by helping him secure the pleasure, or by speaking, helpfully or otherwise, of his pleasure, *his* sensual pleasure may constitute part of the cause of *my* coping with it, and, more specifically, of my referring to it?

BEHAVIORIST: That seems to follow.

SENSUALIST: But in that case the pleasure that he feels and that we both refer to plays an *enabling* role in our shared practice of referring to it. Like tables, pleasures both *support* the behavior that comprises the practice of referring to them and serve—*function*—as the referents of the word ("pleasure") whose meaning is established by this practice.

BEHAVIORIST: So it seems.

SENSUALIST: And cannot pain, itself, constitute at least part of the cause of a man's wincing, groaning, and taking action to relieve the pain?

BEHAVIORIST: Yes.

SENSUALIST: So pain, itself, can constitute at least part of the cause of a man's reporting that he feels the pain?

BEHAVIORIST: Yes.

SENSUALIST: And since I may respond to another person's report by helping to relieve him of his pain, or by speaking, helpfully or not, of it, the occurrence of *his* pain may constitute part of the cause of *my* coping with his pain, and more specifically, his having a pain may constitute part of the cause of my referring to his pain?

BEHAVIORIST: It seems to follow.

SENSUALIST: But in that case the pain that he feels and that we both refer to plays an *enabling* role in our shared practice of referring to it. The pain itself both *supports* the behavior that comprises the practice of referring to it and serves—*functions*—as the referent of the word ("pain") whose meaning is established by this practice.

BEHAVIORIST: So it seems.

SENSUALIST: But is there any reason to think that the case changes when we move from pleasure and pain to the visual impression of the color, scarlet?

BEHAVIORIST: Yes. There is in our behavior no natural expression of a visual impression.

SENSUALIST: True. But once language has got under way, this surely does not prevent the repeated occurrence of visual impressions of scarlet from constituting part of the cause of a man's first learning to report and then continuing to report that he has, from time to time, this very impression?

BEHAVIORIST: Certainly not.

SENSUALIST: So, without my repeating the remarks about enabling role, and about function as referent, you can see that with other sensory experiences we get the same result we got for pleasure and pain, and for tables and chairs: these sensory experiences enter into the use and hence comprise a part of the meaning of the words that serve to refer to them—in case meaning is use, as you hold.

BEHAVIORIST: It begins to seem so.

SENSUALIST: But that is what I set out to prove.

BEHAVIORIST: Yes. And I do not feel well.

SENSUALIST: I know what you mean.

University of Maryland

What We Believe

ALAN R. WHITE

WHAT do we believe when we believe that p, e.g., that there is a life after death or that our last moment has come?

I

The usual answer[1] is that we believe the *proposition* (that) p. Indeed, a proposition is sometimes defined[2] as what is believed (or disbelieved, doubted, assumed, etc.); while, conversely, belief, doubt, suspicion, assumption, etc., are often called "propositional attitudes." Such a definition of "proposition" is, incidentally, inconsistent with another definition commonly made by the same philosophers that a proposition is the meaning of a sentence. We do not believe, doubt, or assume the meanings of sentences, nor is it meanings which are true or false, categorical or conditional, equivalent to or the contradictory of each other.

Certainly, for some V, if somebody Vs that p, then what is Ved is the proposition that p, e.g., if he asserts or states that p; but equally for some V, if somebody Vs that p, what is Ved is not the proposition that p, e.g., if he suspects, fears, or hopes that p. We cannot, therefore, assume that just because A believes that p, what he believes is the proposition that p. This must be argued for or against.

I would like to suggest several plausible but, in my opinion, misleading and mistaken sources of the usual view that to believe that p is to believe the proposition that p.

1. The view seems to gain support from the fact that we undoubtedly often do believe propositions; for instance, when we believe somebody's story, statement, or account, when we believe whatever we hear, read, or are told or when we believe a rumour or propaganda. But although believing the statement or rumour that p entails

[1] E.g., H. H. Price, *Belief* (New York, 1969), p. 38 *et passim*; B. Russell, *An Enquiry into Meaning and Truth* (London, 1940), *passim*; G. E. Moore, *Some Main Problems of Philosophy* (New York, 1962), ch. 3, contrast pp. 263–266; *Lectures on Philosophy* (New York, 1966), ch. xv, Sect. 3, pp. 132–149. Cp. Hume, *Treatise* Bk. I, ch. 3, Sect. vii; Locke, *Essay* Bk. IV.

[2] Cp. L. S. Stebbing, *A Modern Introduction to Logic* (London, 1946), p. 33; Moore, *op. cit.*

believing that p, believing that p does not entail, much less is it the same as, believing the statement or rumour that p, since one can believe that p even if there is no such statement or rumour.

More importantly, believing that p is in many respects quite unlike believing the statement or rumour that p just as it is unlike believing the author of such a statement or rumour. Indeed, we might say that *that p* is quite a different kind of accusative of "believe" from *the proposition that p* or *the author of the statement that p*. The difference between believing, on the one hand, the proposition that p or the author of the statement that p and believing, on the other, that p itself is the same as the difference between suspecting the butler and suspecting foul play, diagnosing a patient and diagnosing tuberculosis, doubting a man (or his word) and doubting his sanity, fearing a teacher (or his temper) and fearing a hiding, advising a trade union and advising a return to work, believing in one's party and believing in fairies. This difference in accusatives has been obscured by the philosophical tendency to refer to both as the *object* of that which is signified by the corresponding verb '*V*', perhaps because both can be said to be *what* is *V*ed. Outside of philosophy, it is the butler, not foul play, that is the object of one's suspicion; a man's word, not his sanity, that is the object of one's doubt; a teacher's temper, not a hiding, that is the object of one's fear; a man or his story, not that p, that is the object of belief. This is because the former are genuine objects which may present themselves to us for some attitude, emotion, action, etc., on our part.

The difference between these two kinds of accusative—which I shall call the "ob ect-accusative," e.g., when I suspect the butler or believe his story, and the "intentional-accusative," e.g., when I suspect foul play or believe that p—is shown in several ways.

First, the intentional-accusative, but not the object-accusative, has an equivalent nominalization form "that p." Suspecting foul play, diagnosing tuberculosis, and advising a return to work amount to suspecting that there is foul play, diagnosing that there is tuberculosis, and advising that there be a return to work; but suspecting the butler, diagnosing a patient, and advising a trade union do not amount to suspecting that there is a butler, diagnosing that there is a patient, and advising that there be a trade union. Similarly, believing in fairies amounts to believing that there are fairies; but believing in one's party does not amount to, even though it implies, believing that there is one's party.

Secondly, the object-accusative, but not the intentional-accusative, must signify something which exists. One can believe or suspect that there is a life after death, and believe in fairies or suspect tuberculosis, although it is not the case that there is a life after death, or fairies, or tuberculosis; but one cannot believe or suspect a person or his story unless he or it exists.

Thirdly, when I believe that there is a life after death, that there is a life after death is my belief, just as when I suspect that there has been foul play and diagnose that my patient has tuberculosis, that there has been foul play is my suspicion and that my patient has tuberculosis is my diagnosis, or just as when I fear a hiding or advise a return to work, a hiding is my fear and a return to work is my advice. But when I believe a man or his story, neither he nor his story is my belief any more than when I suspect the butler, diagnose my patient, or advise a trade union is the butler my suspicion, the patient my diagnosis, or the trade union my advice.

Fourthly, to believe someone or his story, unlike believing that p, is not to believe correctly or erroneously, much less is it to have a correct or erroneous belief. That which one believes when one believes a story may be true or false, scurrilous or amusing, just as the person whom one believes when one believes a person may be male or female, but one does not thereby have a true or false, scurrilous or amusing, belief any more than one has a male or female belief. This is not, of course, to deny that when one believes a person or his story one will also acquire a belief that p and, therefore, when one believes a liar or his false story one will also acquire a false belief that p. To continue or cease to believe someone or his story, unlike believing that p, is not to stick to or revise one's belief.

Fifthly, what is disbelieved, mistrusted, or viewed with skepticism is, and is only, a person or what he says. One does not disbelieve that the earth is flat or that there is a life after death. To be credulous is to be too prone to believe people and their stories; it is not to be too prone to believe that p and that q. To be superstitious, on the other hand, is to believe in the supernatural rather than to believe stories about the supernatural.

Finally, just as suspecting the butler, as contrasted with suspecting foul play, is feeling suspicious of the butler and advising a trade union, as contrasted with advising a return to work, is giving advice to a trade union,[3] so believing a man or his story, as contrasted with believing that p, is putting some trust in him or his story.

2. A related source of the view that when someone believes that p what is believed is a proposition lies in a mistaken analysis of inten-

---

[3] Note the ambiguity in, e.g., "to advise a new Vice-Chancellor" between giving advice to one and advising that there be one.

tional concepts. When faced with intentional concepts, such as those expressed by "imagine," "fear," or "recall," philosophers[4] sometimes used to analyse them in such a way that what was imagined, feared, or recalled when one imagines, fears, or recalls either X or that p was not X or that p itself, but the thought of X or that p, sometimes in the former case called the *concept* X and in the latter the *proposition* p. Thus, it was alleged that what we imagine is not a centaur but the image of a centaur, what we fear is not a visit to the dentist but the thought of such a visit, and what we recall is not the day of our wedding but a memory image of it. The underlying reasons for this analysis were twofold: (i) the supposed impossibility that anything could be Ved (e.g., imagined, feared, or recalled) if or when it did not exist; and (ii) the psychological fact that imagination, fear, and recall are commonly—or, as it was sometimes held, invariably—accompanied by the thought or image of what is imagined, feared, or recalled.

This analysis was then applied to the belief that p and to the belief in X, since it is possible, as in the case of erroneous belief, to believe that p, e.g., that the earth is flat, and to believe in X, e.g., fairies, when what is believed is not so or what is believed in does not exist. Furthermore, it was usually also held that when one believes that p, one also has the thought that p—or, as it was commonly called, "entertains the proposition that p"—in the same way that, supposedly, one has the concept or image of a fairy when one believes in fairies.

But if the analysis of *belief that p* and *belief in X* is to assimilate, as I think it can be, to the analysis of these intentional concepts, then the falsity of the above analysis of intentional concepts implies the falsity of this analysis of the concepts of *belief that p* and of *belief in X*. And such an analysis of intentional concepts is undoubtedly false. There is no reason at all why one cannot imagine, fear, or recall what does not exist or is not so just as one can look for or forbid it. Equally there is no reason why one cannot believe what is not so or believe in what does not exist. Indeed, just as what one believes in when one believes in X cannot be the concept of X, since, according to this theory, this concept must exist, whereas what one believes in need not exist, so the fact that what one believes when one believes that p need not be something which exists suggests that what one believes in this case cannot be the proposition that p,[5] since, according to this

[4] E.g., Moore's opponents in *Some Main Problems of Philosophy*, *op. cit.*, ch. XIII.

[5] Although R. M. Chisholm, "Sentences about Believing," *Proceedings of the Aristotelian Society*, vol. 56 (1956), pp. 125–148, holds that "believe" is intentional, he assumes that what is believed is a proposition.

theory, when one believes that p, the proposition that p undoubtedly does and must exist. This awkward consequence has been overlooked because the fact that one can believe what is not so has been assimilated, as we shall see, to the fact that one can believe what is not true. And since whenever one believes what is not true, one nevertheless believes a proposition, albeit a false proposition, it was thought that whenever one believes what is not so, one believes a proposition.

Furthermore, just as the false analysis of intentional concepts confused the thoughts (concepts, images, propositions) which one often —or, as it was wrongly supposed, invariably—has in imagining, fearing, or recalling X or that p with what is imagined, feared, or recalled, so this false analysis of *belief* has confused the proposition which is commonly—or, as it was wrongly supposed, invariably— "entertained" when one believes that p with what is believed when one believes that p. If, however, belief that p, like belief in X, is analysed as intentional, then there is no reason why what one believes when one believes that p should not be that p itself, even though, when one's belief is erroneous, it is not the case that p; just as what one believes in when one believes in X is X itself, even when X does not exist.

3. A third source of the view that it is a proposition that is believed when one believes that p may be a preoccupation with the perfectly correct point that any answer of the form "that p" to the question "What do you believe?" is given by giving a form of words; and, moreover, a form of words capable of expressing a proposition. But it no more follows from this that what is said to be believed is a proposition, much less a form of words, than it follows from the fact that an answer to the question "What do you see (or build)?" is given by giving a form of words—and, moreover, a form of words capable of expressing a concept—that what is seen or built is a concept or a word. Nor should we allow the view under discussion to borrow credence from the fact that we commonly express our belief that p in the words "that p" or in the proposition that p. We also commonly express our fear, suspicion, or hope that p in these words or in this proposition too; but this does not allow us to say that what we fear, suspect, or hope is a set of words or a proposition.

4. A fourth source of the view under discussion may be our habit of expressing *A believes that p* as *A believes p*, e.g., "He believes that there is a life after death" as "He believes there is a life after death." From this philosophers move in several mistaken ways. First, they simply jump to the conclusion that 'p' in "A believes p" indicates a proposition. Secondly, they assimilate the elliptical form "A believes

F

p" to "*A* believes *X*" where *X* is, e.g., a person or his story and wrongly conclude that what holds for "*A* believes *X*" holds for "*A* believes *p*." Thirdly, they suppose that "*A* believes *p*" is elliptical for "*A* believes *p* to be true" in the way that "*A* believes the proposition *p*" may be elliptical for "*A* believes the proposition *p* to be true," and "*A* believes the person *B*" for "*A* believes the person *B* to be telling the truth." From this they argue that since what can be true (or false) is a proposition, then '*p*' in "*A* believes *p*" indicates a proposition and, hence, that what is believed when *A* believes *p* is a proposition. To this argument there are, however, several objections.

First, "*A* believes *p*" is not elliptical for "*A* believes *p* to be true." On the one hand, "*A* believes *p* to be true" is strictly nonsense, as is clear when an example is substituted for '*p*', e.g., "*A* believes there is a life after death to be true." On the other hand to interpret "*A* believes *p* to be true" as "*A* believes the proposition *p* to be true," though giving a perfectly sensible statement similar to "*A* believes *B*'s story to be true," is to beg the question whether "*A* believes *p*" is the same as "*A* believes the proposition *p*."

Incidentally, even if "*A* believes the proposition (or story) *p*" is elliptical for "*A* believes the proposition (or story) *p* to be true," and "*A* believes the person *B*" is elliptical for "*A* believes the person *B* to be telling the truth," one cannot in general argue that there is a legitimate form "*A* believes *X*" which is elliptical for "*A* believes *X* to be *Y*." It is clear that if one believes a proposition to be false or a person to be lying, one does not believe the proposition or the person, nor, if one believes a gearbox to be faulty or working well, one does believe the gearbox. What or who is said to be believed in "*A* believes *X* to be *Y*" is not *X*[6] any more than what or who is said to be known, suspected, discovered, or understood in "*A* knows, suspects, discovers, or understands *X* to be *Y*" is *X*. This is a way in which "*A* believes (knows, suspects, discovers, understands) *X* to be *Y*" is different from, e.g., "*A* advises or forces *X* to be *Y*," where *X* is, indeed, what or who is said to be advised or forced.[7] An equivalent of "*A* believes *X* to be *Y*" is, perhaps, "*A* believes that *X* is *Y*," but neither the legitimate form "*A* advises that *X* should be *Y*" nor, much less, the illegitimate form "*A* advises that *X* is *Y*" is equivalent

[6] A. N. Prior, "Oratio Obliqua," *Proceedings of the Aristotelian Society Supplementary Vol.* 38 (1963), pp. 115–126 seems to suppose it sometimes is, on the grounds that if *A* believes something of *X*, then *X* is the object of which *A* believes something.

[7] *Pace* M. Kiteley, "The Grammars of 'believe'," *The Journal of Philosophy*, vol. 61 (1964), p. 249 who wrongly assimilates "*A* thought *X* (to be) *Y*" to "*A* appointed *X* (to be) *Y*."

to "*A* advises *X* to be *Y*." Further, if *A* believes (suspects, discovers, understands) *X* to be a supporter of *Y*, then, conversely, *A* believes (suspects, discovers, understands) *Y* to be supported by *X*; but if *A* advises or forces *X* to be a supporter of *Y*, it does not follow that *A* advises or forces *Y* to be supported by *X*.

Secondly, "*A* believes the proposition *S is P* to be true," e.g., "*A* believes the proposition that the gearbox is faulty to be true," is not the same as, though it may be logically equivalent to, "*A* believes *S* to be *P*," e.g., "*A* believes the gearbox to be faulty"; nor, similarly, is "*A* believes that it is true that *p*," e.g., "*A* believes that it is true that there is a life after death," the same as—though it may be logically equivalent to—"*A* believes that *p*," e.g., "*A* believes that there is a life after death." To suppose these are the same is like supposing that "it is true that *p*," e.g., "It is true that there is a life after death" is the same as—because it may be logically equivalent to—*p*, e.g., "There is a life after death," or that "*A* fears, expects, or complains that *p*" is the same as "*A* fears, expects, or complains that it is true that *p*." Indeed, if the belief that *p* were the same as the belief that it is true that *p*, we would be on the slippery slope of an infinite regress, for the belief that *p* would then be the belief that *q*, namely, that it is true that *p*, which would itself be the belief that *r*, namely, that it is true that *q*, namely that it is true that *p*; and the belief that *r* would be. . . .

Thirdly, even if "*A* believes that *p*" were the same as "*A* believes that it is true that *p*," this would not show that what is said to be believed is in either case a proposition. It is, of course, correct that what is true is a proposition, but what is said to be believed in "*A* believes that it is true that *p*" is not that *p* at all, but that *q*, namely, that it is true that *p*, just as what is said to be believed in "*A* believes that it is false that *p*" is not that *p*, but that *r*, namely, that it is false that *p*. There is no more reason to suppose that because what is said to be true in "It is true that *p*" is the proposition that *p*, therefore what is said to be believed in "*A* believes that *p*" is also the proposition that *p* than there would be to suppose that because what is said to be true in "*A* fears that it is true that *p*" is the proposition that *p*, therefore what is said to be feared in "*A* fears that *p*" is the proposition that *p* and, therefore *A* fears a proposition. Nor, indeed, does any of this show that what is said to be believed (or feared) in "*A* believes (or fears) that it is true that *p*" is the proposition that it is true that *p*.

5. A fifth and minor source of confusion may be the assimilation,[8]

[8] E.g., Price, *op. cit., passim.*

perhaps initiated by Newman, between believing something and assenting to something. It may well be that what one commonly assents to, dissents from, accepts, entertains, or rejects is a proposition or proposal, plan, or suggestion. But, significantly, one does not assent to, dissent from, entertain, or reject that *p*.

6. My final suggestion of a mistaken source for the assimilation of *believing that p* with *believing the proposition that p* is a parallel mistaken assimilation of *knowing that p* with *knowing the proposition that p*.

Belief is commonly contrasted by philosophers with *knowledge* on the grounds that what is believed can be true or false but what is known can only be true. Since it is propositions which can be either true or false and propositions which can be only true, it is concluded that what is believed, and what is known, is a proposition. But there is a confusion here. The fact that the truth of the proposition "He believes that *p*" does not depend, while the truth of the proposition "He knows that *p*" does depend, on the truth of the proposition that *p* does not show that what he believes when he believes that *p* or what he knows when he knows that *p* is a proposition anymore than the fact that the truth of the proposition "He fears that *p*" does not depend, while the truth of the proposition "He discovers that *p*" does depend, on the truth of the proposition that *p* shows that what he fears when he fears that *p* and what he discovers when he discovers that *p* is a proposition. The fact that the propositions "He knew that the earth was flat" and "The earth is not flat" are contrary does not show that what he thought he knew, namely that the earth is flat and what is so, namely that the earth is not flat, are propositions any more than the fact that the propositions "He knew a fairy" and "There are no fairies" are contrary shows that what he thought he knew but does not exist is not a fairy, but perhaps only the concept of a fairy. Furthermore, the correct distinction between what is believed, when it is believed that *p*, and what is known, when it is known that *p*, is not between what can be either true or false and what can be only true but between what can be either so or not so and what can only be so. This is partly recognized by those philosophers who, although often speaking of knowing propositions, also speak more correctly of knowing facts. But unless facts are identified as or with true propositions—a misidentification which some philosophers[9] make —the admission that what is known are facts entails—as the Meinong-Russell-Moore worries about false propositions, facts, etc. some fifty years ago made plain—either that the sorts of things which are

[9] See references and discussion in A. R. White, *Truth* (New York, 1970).

correctly believed, allegedly true propositions, are not the sorts of things which are known, admittedly facts, or that what we believe correctly is a fact and only what we believe incorrectly is a proposition, namely a false proposition. The first alternative, however, flies in the face of our conviction that what is believed when it is correctly believed that *p* is the same as what is known when it is known that *p*, while the second alternative forces us to hold that what some people correctly believe cannot be the same sort of thing as what other people erroneously believe.

The confusion here between believing (or knowing) something to be *so* and believing (or knowing) something to be *true* is no doubt due to the fact that it is true that *p* if and only if *p*. But this truism must not blind us to the difference between what *is* true (or false), namely the proposition that *p*, and what *makes* it true (or false), namely that fact that *p*. The alleged platitude[10] that if someone knows that *p*, then it is true that *p* is a platitude not because what is known is a true proposition, but because if someone knows that *p*, then it is a fact that *p* and if it is a fact that *p* then it is true (to say) that *p*. To say, e.g., "*A* fears, expects, suspects, discovers, notices, is surprised, understands that it is true that *p*" is different from saying, e.g., "*A* fears, expects, suspects, discovers, notices, is surprised, understands that *p*." It may be that philosophers have been misled because their experience as disputants has been more to do with whether or not to believe that certain statements, theories, or hypotheses which have been put before them are true than with whether or not to believe that certain things are so.

If *that p* in "*A* believes that *p*" and "*A* knows that *p*" were elliptical for *the proposition that p*, then the common thesis that if *A* knows that *p*, then *A* believes that *p* would become the thesis that if *A* knows the proposition that *p*, then *A* believes the proposition that *p*. But this latter thesis has none of the plausibility of the former and is, indeed, no better than the obviously mistaken thesis that if *A* knows the rumour that *p*, then *A* believes the rumour that *p* or than the thesis that if *A* knows the author of the rumour that *p*, then *A* believes the author of the rumour that *p*. In short, "*A* knows that *p*" does not mean "*A* knows the proposition that *p*."

II

The thesis that what is believed when one believes that *p* is not a proposition, but a form of words, e.g., the sentence '*p*', has not very

[10] Cp. Price, *op. cit.*, p. 79.

commonly been held. Indeed, it is its obvious faults that historically provided one of the main reasons for the thesis that what is believed is a proposition, just as the view that what is true or false is a proposition was partly due to dissatisfaction with the view that the bearer of truth or falsity is a sentence. Conversely, most modern advocates of the view that what is believed is a form of words seem persuaded of this soley because of their further conviction that so called propositions are really sentences.[11]

The objections to this latter view are well known and need not be repeated here.[12] They seem to me clearly valid. The thesis that what is believed is a sentence is open to analogous objections either when what is believed is that p or when it is the proposition (story, etc.) that p. It is absurd to suppose that French and English believers either in a life after death or in the doctrine of a life after death believe different things, one a French and the other an English sentence. The sentence "There is a life after death" may be grammatical, inelegant, or English; but these are not characteristics of what is believed. Conversely, what is believed, but not a sentence, can either be something which is unlikely, impossible, or not so or it can be a false story or an exaggerated rumour. Even to believe every word an Englishman says—which I have just argued is different from believing that p—is not to believe English words, but what is expressed in English words.

III

A more recent and more radical answer to the question "What is it that is believed when one believes that p?" is "Nothing." For, according to this view, "believe" does not signify a relation between a believer and what he believes nor does "that p" name what he believes.

1. One reason for this view occurs in Moore's *Some Main Problems of Philosophy*.[13] Dissatisfied—rightly in my opinion—with his early view that what is believed is necessarily a proposition, Moore reached the conclusion that "that p" refers to the fact that p. But since in an erroneous belief there is no fact that p, Moore felt obliged to hold

[11] E.g., W. V. Quine, *Word and Object* (New York, 1960), Sect. 44; R. Carnap, *Meaning and Necessity* (Illinois, 1967), pp. 54–55, 61–62; cp. A. Kenny, "Oratio Obliqua," *Proceedings of the Aristotelian Society, Supplementary Vol.* 37 (1963), pp. 127–146.

[12] Cp. White, *op. cit.*, ch. 1, Sect. b (ii).

[13] *Op. cit.*, pp. 263–266, 291 ff.

that, at least in these cases, "that p"—and similarly 'X' in "A wrongly believes in X"—does not name anything, since he thought it cannot name what does not exist. Nor, for the same reason, can "believes" or "believes in" signify a relation between the believer and what he believes, namely the fact that p or X. As Moore put it, "Whenever we entertain a false belief, there really is, in a sense, no such thing as *what* we believe in."

There are, however, at least three mistakes in this argument. First, as we have seen, it is a peculiarity of any intentional verb V that one can VX or V that p even when there is no X nor is it the case that p. Hence, if *believe*, like *believe in* or like *imagine*—both of which Moore treated similarly in the same context—is intentional, there is something which we believe when we believe that p, whether or not it is the case that p. Secondly, "that p" or 'X' can be used to refer to, e.g., the fact (or state of affairs) that p or the object X even when there is no fact (a state of affairs) that p or no object X. Thirdly, a set of words does not have to be a name of something in order to be used to refer to something which can be an object. "A man in a brown coat" can refer to an object in "He hit a man in a brown coat," but it is not in any narrow sense a name.[14]

2. A second, very recently given, reason for this negative thesis depends on the grammatical conjecture that "believes" in "A believes that p" is intransitive and that, therefore, "that p" is not an accusative of "believes." Such a conjecture, however, runs contrary to the view held by grammarians themselves and seems inconsistent with the fact that "believe" can take the passive and the cleft version transformations, which are signs of transitivity.[15] Nor do the arguments advanced in favor of the conjecture seem to be valid.

(a) One argument[16] for the intransitivity of "believe" is interestingly related to the traditional view that what is believed is a proposition. This argument assumes that "believe," and also "suspect" and "fear," can be transitive only if what is believed, suspected, or feared is a proposition, as when I believe a man's story. Rightly accepting that it is not a proposition that is believed, suspected, or feared when one believes, suspects, or fears that p, the argument

---

[14] Cp. Kenny, *op. cit.* and B. Rundle, "Transitivity and Indirect Speech," *Proceedings of the Aristotelian Society*, vol. 68 (1968), pp. 187–206; contrast Prior, *op. cit.*, and Kiteley, *op. cit.*

[15] Cp. N. Chomsky, *Syntactic Structures* (The Hague, 1965), pp. 42–43; P. S. Rosenbaum, *The Grammar of English Predicate Complement Constructions* (Cambridge, Mass., 1967), pp. 113–114; R. B. Lees, *The Grammar of English Nominalizations* (Bloomington, Ind., 1960), pp. 59–60, 64; Rundle, *op. cit.*, p. 199.

[16] E.g. Rundle, *op. cit.*, pp. 202–203.

concludes that in these cases the verbs are intransitive. But the assumption in this argument simply begs the question in regard to "believes" and makes the implausible assertion that "fears" in "*A* fears that *p*" is intransitive.

(b) A second argument[17] for the intransitivity of "believes" in "*A* believes that *p*" is the allegation that the correct parsing of "*A* believes that *p*" is not, as is commonly assumed, "*A* believes that-*p*," but rather "*A* believes-that *p*," where "believes-that" does not express a relation between *A* and something else of which '*p*' is the name. Such an argument, however, seems to be a grammatical error.[18] First, the "that" in "*A* believes that *p*" can be legitimately and commonly omitted to give "*A* believes *p*," e.g., "*A* believes (that) there is a life after death." Secondly, both the passive and the cleft version transformations suggest that the "that" goes properly with '*p*' and not with "believes." Thus, we say "That *p* is believed by *A*" and "What *A* believes is that *p*" rather than "*p* is believed-that by *A*" and "What *A* believes-that is *p*." Thirdly, the connection of the "that" with '*p*' rather than with the verb is parallelled by verbs which take a variety of accusatives. Thus, just as we transform "*A* knows that *p*" into the passive "That *p* is known by *A*" rather than "*p* is known-that by *A*" and into the cleft version "What *A* knows is that *p*" rather than "What *A* knows-that is *p*," so we transform "*A* knows how to *V* or where *X* is" into "How to *V* or where *X* is is known by *A*" rather than "*V* is known-how-to by *A* or *X* is known-where by *A*" and into "What *A* knows is how to *V* or where *X* is" rather than "What *A* knows-how-to is *V* or what *A* knows-where is *X*." Fourthly, where a following word does properly belong[19] to the verb rather than to the accusative, as in "*A* believes *in X*," the passive version is "*X* is believed-in by *A*" rather than "In *X* is believed by *A*" and the cleft version is "What *A* believes-in is *X*" rather than "What *A* believes is in *X*."

(c) A third argument[20] in support of the view that "believes" in "*A* believes that *p*" is intransitive and, hence, that "that *p*" is not an accusative of "believes" relies on the fact that "believes" can be used

[17] E.g., Prior, *op. cit.*; Quine, *op. cit.*

[18] Rundle, *op. cit.*, p. 188 seems, wrongly, to accept Prior's premiss, though he queries that the conclusion follows. On the synonymity of active and passive, cp. e.g., J. J. Katz and E. Martin, "The Synonymy of Actives and Passives," *The Philosophical Review*, vol. 76 (1967), pp. 76–91; contrast P. Ziff, "The Non-synonymy of Active and Passive Sentences," *The Philosophical Review*, vol. 75 (1966), pp. 226–232.

[19] Kiteley, *op. cit.*, p. 244 seems to suppose the opposite.

[20] E.g., Kiteley, *op. cit.*, pp. 252–255; Rundle, *op. cit.*, pp. 194–195, 203–204.

parenthetically, as in "No one, he believed, was left alive." But there does not seem to be any necessary connection between being parenthetical and being intransitive. Are the parenthetical verbs intransitive in "No one, he noticed, saw, knew, was left alive" or in " 'No one,' he wrote, whispered, muttered, scrawled, typed, 'was left alive' ?"

(d) A fourth argument advanced for the intransitivity of "believe" is this: Because someone who believes that p has a belief that p just as much as someone who firmly or tentatively believes has a firm or tentative belief, when "belief" is an *internal* accusative of "believe," it has been said[21] that "that p" might "plausibly be called an adjective of internal accusatives, and thus be assigned adverbial force." It is then concluded that "believe" is intransitive and that "that p," like "firm" or "tentative," indicates *how* someone believes rather than *what* he believes. This argument rightly, in my opinion, distinguishes between the kind of accusative signified by "that p" in "*A* believes that p" and the kind of accusative signified by "the man," "the man's story," or "the proposition that p" in "*A* believes the man, the man's story, or the proposition that p." These two kinds of accusative are, as we saw in Section I, just as different as those in "*A* suspects foul play" and "*A* suspects the butler." But the argument's analysis of the former kind of accusative seems to me mistaken. To see this we have to examine the notion of an internal accusative.

A host of verbs has both an internal and an external accusative; where the internal accusative is a verbal noun characterizing what is Ved by reference to the Ving of it, but being itself identifiable by reference to the external accusative, that is, what is Ved. For example, if one bequeaths or discovers something, then there is something one makes, called a "bequest" or "discovery," and something one makes it of, e.g., a house or gold, which is, also called a "bequest" or "discovery." One does not, however, bequeath the bequest (or discover the discovery) one makes,[22] even though both what one makes and what one makes it of, e.g., a bequest of a house (a discovery of gold) can be called a bequest (a discovery). As something made, a bequest can be generous, sensible, or illegal; as what is bequeathed, it can be something brick, rambling, or Georgian. Hence, a man can bequeath generously, sensibly or illegally, but not brickly, ramblingly, or Georgianly. A house's existence as a house, unlike its existence as a bequest, is independent of its being bequeathed; but the existence of a bequest is totally dependent on its being made.

An exact analogy to all this occurs with *believe*—and also with a host of other "mental" verbs, such as *assume, suspect, diagnose, fear*. When someone believes, assumes, suspects, diagnoses, or fears that *p* or believes in, assumes, suspects, diagnoses, or fears *X*, then there is something he has or makes, called a belief, a belief in, a suspicion, fear, assumption, or diagnosis, and something which he believes, believes in, assumes, suspects, diagnoses, or fears, also sometimes called a belief, assumption, suspicion, diagnosis, or fear, namely that *p* or *X*. But he does not believe the belief, assume the assumption, suspect the suspicion, diagnose the diagnosis, or fear the fear which he has or makes, nor does he have or make the belief, assumption, suspicion, diagnosis, or fear, namely that *p* or *X*, which is what he believes, assumes, suspects, diagnoses, or fears; even though both what he has and what he has it of can be called a belief (suspicion, etc.) and, perhaps, "What does he believe (suspect, etc.)?" can be used as a request both for his belief (suspicion, etc.) and what it is of. Only the belief, or belief in, that someone has or the diagnosis he makes can be erroneous, sensible, tentative, or revised; while only what he believes, believes in or diagnoses can be something likely, impossible, non-existent, or about to happen. Hence, someone can believe or diagnose erroneously, sensibly, tentatively, or subject to revision, but not likely, impossibly, or non-existently. A belief, but not what is believed, can be mine or yours. It is because what *A* believes or suspects is so that *A*'s belief or suspicion is correct. Fears and suspicions, unlike what is feared or suspected, can be awakened or subside, be conquered or suppressed. What is believed, suspected or feared exists as a belief, suspicion, or fear only in so far and as long as it is believed, suspected, or feared, but its existence as something else, e.g., as life after death, or as the fact that there is a life after death, is independent of its existence as a belief, suspicion, or fear. The existence of the belief, suspicion, or fear which is had is, on the contrary, wholly dependent on its being had. Nor could one have a belief (belief in, suspicion, or fear) unless there was something, existent or non-existent, which one believed (believed in, suspected, or feared) any more than one could make a bequest or a discovery, unless there was something one bequeathed or discovered. Further, the belief, suspicion, or fear one has, namely the belief that *p* or the belief in *X*, is describable by reference to what one believes, suspects, or fears, namely that *p* or *X*, just as the bequest or discovery one makes is describable by reference to what one bequeaths or discovers.

Hence, knowing what someone's bequest or belief is involves knowing what he bequeaths or believes, and *vice versa*. A list of one's beliefs, fears, or hopes is necessarily a list of what one believes, fears, or hopes just as a list of one's bequests, discoveries, likes, and dislikes is a list of what one bequeaths, discovers, likes, and dislikes.

The important points to be stressed in all this are, first, that what is believed, even if it is called a belief, is quite different from the belief which is had or entertained; and, secondly, that one cannot have a belief (a belief in, a suspicion, etc.) unless there is something other than the belief (belief in, suspicion) to play the role of that which is believed (believed in, suspected). Hence, the fact that "that *p*" can be an adjective of the internal accusative "belief" is no reason for supposing that it cannot also be the name of the intentional accusative, which expresses what is believed. It would be ridiculous to argue that just because a man who firmly and sincerely believes in fairies holds a firm, sincere, and in-fairies belief, therefore "fairies" cannot also be the name of what he believes in. The above argument, based on the notion of an internal accusative, is no better than this.

As the traditional view failed to distinguish between *believing that p* and *believing the proposition that p,* so this view fails to distinguish between *the belief that p* and *what is believed,* namely, *that p.*

IV

If, then, what is believed when one believes that *p*, e.g., that there is a life after death or that one's last moment has come, is neither a proposition nor a sentence nor merely nothing, what is it? I am not sure that there is any general answer[23] to this, except that it is something which exists when the belief is not mistaken and does not exist when it is mistaken, just as what is believed in when one believes in *X*, is *X* itself and not a concept, word or nothing, even when *X* does not exist. In other words, *believe* is used intentionally in *believe that p* and, sometimes, in *believe in X*.

One argument for this answer is the analogy between *believe that p* and *believe in X* which is comparable to the analogy between suspecting, diagnosing, or fearing that the patient has tuberculosis and suspecting, diagnosing, or fearing tuberculosis. Often the belief that *p*, e.g., that there are fairies or a life after death, implies and is

---

[23] In the great majority of cases (e.g., "tell," "discover," "don't care," "it is a mystery," "irrelevant"; contrast, "express," "prove") the "what" of "what he believes" is interrogative, not relative.

implied by the belief in X, e.g., in fairies or a life after death, just as the suspicion, diagnosis, or fear that the patient has tuberculosis implies and is implied by the suspicion, diagnosis, or fear of tuberculosis in the patient.[24]

The University, Hull

[24] I am indebted for comments on an earlier draft to Peter Geach, William Kneale, Gilbert Ryle, Aaron Sloman, Christopher Williams, and my colleagues at Hull.

INDEX OF NAMES

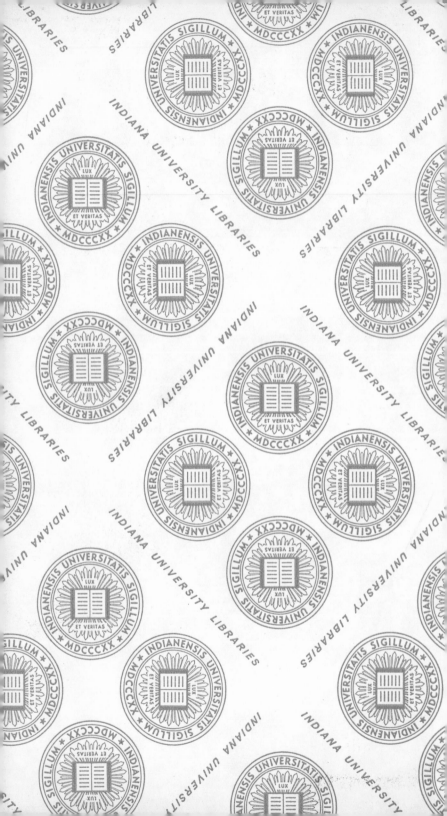